HAUNTED GETTYSBURG

PARANORMAL TALES *from* *the* FIELD *of* BATTLE

BARRY CORBETT

AMERICA
THROUGH
TIME

For Sylvia, my Grandmother
who encouraged me to take risks.

America Through Time®
An imprint of Sutton Publishing Inc.
www.through-time.com

First published 2025

ISBN 978-1-63499-560-3

Typeset in Sabon
Printed and bound in England

Contents

ACKNOWLEDGMENTS

I would like to thank Loring Schultz, Jr. and Cynthia Codori-Schultz of the Farnsworth House Inn for their first-hand stories and the use of their spirit photography; Krystle Kitchen and Glenn Hart, Jr. for the use of their photography at the Brickhouse Inn; Jeremy and Danielle Davis of the Cashtown Inn for their personal stories and warm hospitality; Jenu Six and Chantal Lynn of "The Old Souls" for the use of their photography at the National Soldiers' Orphans Homestead; Paul Lucas and Lourdes Vicente for the use of her photography at the Triangular Field; Lynn Light Heller for the use of her photography at the Jacob Weikert farm; and Brian Codagnone for historical consultation.

Photographs of Old Dorm and the Hummelbaugh farmhouse courtesy of Deposit Stock Photo. Photograph of the George Weikert farmhouse courtesy of Adobe Stock Photography. Photograph of Stevens Hall courtesy of iStock Photo.

INTRODUCTION

In great deeds, something abides. On great fields, something stays. Forms change and pass; bodies disappear, but spirits linger, to consecrate ground for the vision place of souls.

Col. Joshua Chamberlain
At the dedication of the monument to the 20th Maine
October 1889

I am no stranger to ghosts, having spent the last eight years chasing shadows throughout the New England area with the team at Boston Paranormal Investigators. But the town of Gettysburg seems to display an exceptional variety of paranormal phenomena. Plan a stay at one of the town's charming inns, explore the battlefield and National Park, or spend some time interacting with the townsfolk and you will hear countless tales of spectral wraiths, disembodied spirits, and ghostly apparitions.

It is widely believed that the town is haunted by the discarnate spirits of Civil War-era soldiers, both Union and Confederate. What made this battle unique is that a great portion of it took place among the streets and alleys of the town of Gettysburg. This peaceful hamlet of 2,450 residents found themselves suddenly thrust into the center of a violent and bloody nightmare. Before the battle had ended, there were over sixty makeshift, field hospitals scattered throughout the area, inside taverns, barns, and residential homes. In many instances, the Gettysburg townsfolk pitched in to help stabilize the wounded.

America's Civil War has been well-documented for 160 years, and the Battle of Gettysburg stands among the seminal events in American history. But I am not a historian; I am merely a storyteller. I have chosen to include a number of compelling tales from both the battlefield and the active areas within the town. Many of these stories have been passed along by word of mouth, some are first-hand accounts, others could be relegated to folklore, but it is clear to me that something unearthly has been going on in the hallowed fields of Gettysburg.

General Lee considered the capture of Culp's Hill crucial to Confederate victory.

On July 3, cannon fire lit up the sky as "Pickett's Charge" attacked the center of the Union force on Cemetery Hill. (*Illustration by Kurz and Allison, 1884*)

By the middle of the nineteenth century, mankind had managed to develop new and efficient ways to take human lives. The solid-core, lead musket balls employed for the last three hundred years had been replaced in 1830 by the minie ball, a hollowed-out, lead bullet designed to compress upon impact, essentially exploding into the victim's body, where it caused human bones to shatter into pieces.

Cast-iron cannonballs were improved upon by hollow cannister shells, which contained fifty to sixty smaller lead balls. When fired, the thin shell self-destructed and the deadly shrapnel spread out like a blast from a shotgun, covering a far greater field of impact, and tearing apart life and limb in the process.

Although army surgeons in 1863 had access to powerful anesthetics such as morphine, ether, and chloroform, they were often forced to rely on alcohol when the supply chains were interrupted. The discovery of antibiotics was some sixty years in the future, so the rate of infection was extremely high. For this reason, amputation was the preferred treatment for a serious wound.

Was the suffering at Gettysburg more intense than in previous wars? Was it the sheer scope of the body count in such a short period of time? The battle lasted only three days. Impressionable teenagers as young as fourteen volunteered for the "grand adventure" of fighting for the cause. Perhaps their developing minds could not accept the sudden finality of death. Instead, their spectral forms continue to engage in an endless battle, for all of eternity.

The view from Cemetery Ridge, where the Army of the Potomac made their final stand.

Once the furious battle had ended, the townsfolk went back to their routine lives, but they were now spending those lives amidst a scene of devastation. More than 50,000 soldiers lost their lives at Gettysburg. So many of its combatants endured devastating wounds and suffered the pain of rampant infection, some after surviving horrific amputations.

Is it possible that the sheer magnitude of suffering has infused the very land with its energetic trauma? In the study of the paranormal, we rarely get satisfying answers to our questions. It is virtually impossible to capture compelling evidence that proves the existence of spirits. Ghostly phenomena can be observed, recorded or captured on video, but it is seldom repeatable, and because of this, the spirit world is difficult to analyze by scientific process. If you have seen a ghost, you probably believe in them. If you have not, then you are choosing to rely on second-hand testimony, or you may never be convinced that they exist. In the examination of the worlds beyond the veil, we have only theory and speculation.

Something has endured in Gettysburg. The discarnate consciousness of fallen soldiers appears somehow to have transcended death. Most of these men died in a violent manner, far away from their homes and families, many never to be identified, their bodies torn to shreds, and unceremoniously buried in unmarked gravesites.

One thing is certain: these earth-bound spirits are longing to have their stories told.

Little Round Top forms a spectacular backdrop for a monument to the 4th New York Independent Battery, known as "Smith's Battery."

On the Bloody Wheatfield stands a monument to the 9th Massachusetts Battery.

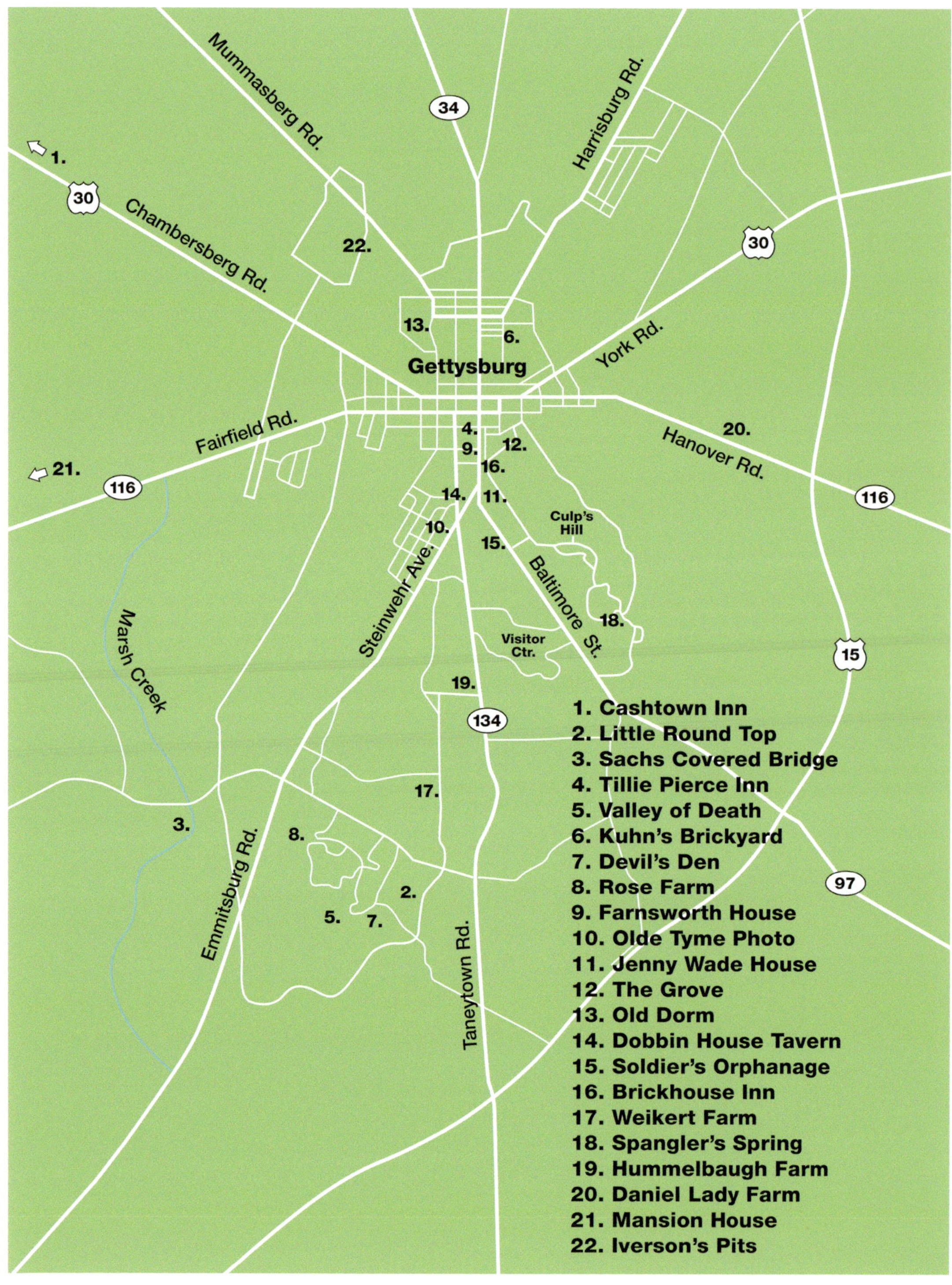
Mummasberg Rd.
34
Harrisburg Rd.
1.
30
Chambersberg Rd.
22.
30
13.
6.
Gettysburg
York Rd.
Fairfield Rd.
4.
9.
12.
20.
Hanover Rd.
21.
116
16.
116
14.
11.
Culp's Hill
10.
15.
Steinwehr Ave.
Baltimore St.
18.
Marsh Creek
Visitor Ctr.
15
19.
134
17.
3.
8.
Emmitsburg Rd.
2.
97
5.
7.
Taneytown Rd.
1. Cashtown Inn
2. Little Round Top
3. Sachs Covered Bridge
4. Tillie Pierce Inn
5. Valley of Death
6. Kuhn's Brickyard
7. Devil's Den
8. Rose Farm
9. Farnsworth House
10. Olde Tyme Photo
11. Jenny Wade House
12. The Grove
13. Old Dorm
14. Dobbin House Tavern
15. Soldier's Orphanage
16. Brickhouse Inn
17. Weikert Farm
18. Spangler's Spring
19. Hummelbaugh Farm
20. Daniel Lady Farm
21. Mansion House
22. Iverson's Pits

1

The Cashtown Inn

If you have come to Gettysburg looking for the ghosts, you are going to love the Cashtown Inn. There is little doubt that it is one of the most haunted venues in the area, even though it is situated 8 miles northwest of the main battle. Built in 1797 to serve as the first stagecoach stop west of Gettysburg, the original inn contained four small but cozy rooms. Since that point it has served many functions, a bar, a tavern, and even a safe house used by escaped slaves traveling the underground railroad.

Before the battle, Confederate General Ambrose Hill met at the Cashtown Inn to discuss tactics with General Robert E. Lee.

In 1815, Peter Marck obtained a license to operate a four-room tavern for weary travelers. Peter replaced the original log structure with a three-story, brick building. Marck was renowned for demanding cash up front, and the name Cashtown stuck. In fact, the inn became so popular that the townsfolk named the nearby village Cashtown.

Marck ran the inn for thirty years and then sold it to Henry Mickley in 1854. Mickley passed it down to his son, Jacob. Shortly after the Civil War, it was purchased by Daniel and Mary Heintzelman. The current owners, Jeremy and Danielle Davis, bought the property in 2021. At the time, they did not believe the paranormal tales associated with the building. Things have changed in the interim.

The Cashtown Inn is most famous for housing Confederate General A. P. Hill during the three-day battle for Gettysburg. A painting by prominent artist Dale Gallon is proudly displayed in the main lobby. It depicts General Robert E. Lee conferring with General Hill in front of the old inn. In June 1863, Lee moved the bulk of his army into southern Pennsylvania. Historians agree that Lee and his 22,000 troops passed by the inn on their way to the battle.

Cashtown would have been strategically located to serve as a Confederate supply line to Virginia. General Hill suffered from chronic kidney disease and needed a secure place where he could enjoy home-cooked meals and regain his strength for the coming battle. The innkeeper at the time, Jacob Mickley later stated: "The entire force under Lee passed within twenty feet of my barroom." He would later bemoan the fact that the defeated Confederate army retraced their steps through Cashtown in retreat, seizing supplies along the way. He claimed to have lost a wagon, a steer, fifty chickens, 100 apple trees, and 480 gallons of whiskey. The damages amounted to $2,000, a vast amount of money in 1863.

The area behind the village was quickly converted into an encampment, and General Hill turned his room at the tavern into the Confederate headquarters, where he met with

Mysterious figures appear at the Cashtown Inn, often staring out of the second-story windows.

Generals Henry Heth, John Imboden, and Commander Robert E. Lee as they planned their strategy. Down in the cellar, the two great firebrick ovens worked around the clock, continuously baking loaves of bread, a valuable commodity for a standing army.

Their stay was cut short. General Imboden sent a battalion of his troops out to search for supplies. Halfway between Cashtown and Gettysburg, the rebel troops encountered a Union infantry brigade, and the first skirmish of the battle had begun. Historians are confident that the first fatality at Gettysburg occurred in Cashtown. General Lee had been gradually massing his troops for the upcoming battle. He had hoped to overwhelm the Union troops and force them northward before they could bring in reinforcements, but General George Meade and the Army of the Potomac had other plans.

General Hill had the basement converted into a field hospital, and for three days, as the crucial battle waged across the surrounding area, hundreds of wounded rebel soldiers were brought in for treatment. With limited resources and no antibiotics, they could only bandage and stabilize the minor injuries. Amputation was their solution for major wounds. As they had done in other triage units throughout the war, field surgeons hacked off arms and legs, employing ether, morphine, and opium as painkillers. Surviving soldiers described a pile of discarded limbs that reached so high that it threatened to blot out the basement windows.

An army in retreat is often forced to transport their wounded, leaving little time for critical care on their trek back to Virginia. Soldiers who could walk were forced to march. The others were loaded onto rickety carts or wagons; many would never make it back to Virginia. It is not surprising that the energy from all that violence and trauma might be infused into the rafters, walls and floorboards of the historic building.

Patrons often hear footsteps, gunshots, and disembodied voices. In fact, there have been so many reports of hauntings that the current owners have placed a journal in each

In the cellar, amputated limbs were casually tossed out of the windows, forming a grisly pile in the yard.

room, allowing visitors to document their paranormal phenomena. One of the previous owners handed each guest a flyer that strongly warned against the use of a Ouija board inside their room. Where else but Gettysburg would you find such an unusual request?

In Room Four, many a night's sleep has been interrupted at two in the morning by three loud raps on the door. Leaping out of bed in terror and throwing open the door, the mystified guests find no sign of their spectral culprit. They return to bed, praying for the dawn to arrive, only to be awakened an hour later by the same phenomenon. Some patrons complain about cold spots and doorknobs that jiggle in the middle of the night. Others have heard footsteps pacing across their rooms, and one guest said the apparition of a rebel soldier sat down on the edge of her bed. She shut her eyes until the ghostly phantom disappeared.

There are five guest rooms at the inn, and each bears the name of a Confederate general: the James Pedigrew, the John Imboden, the A. P. Hill, the Henry Heth, and the Robert E. Lee Suite. A female spirit seems to favor the Imboden room. Her strong perfume has been noted many times by members of the Davis family. In the Hill room, the pungent scent of cigar smoke permeates the area. Perhaps the general was a smoker. And, of course, the cellar is a veritable hotbed of activity. There are few guests brave enough to spend their night in the same area where terrified soldiers spent their last, dying breaths. Full-bodied apparitions have appeared in all areas of the inn but most often in the fieldstone cellar. One Confederate soldier seems very fond of Room Five. He

A hotel guest posed for a photograph in 1895, unaware that a ghostly apparition stood behind him.

has been photographed a few times, standing at attention or peering wistfully out of the windows. Witnesses say he looks like a teenager, and there is testimony that soldiers as young as twelve had volunteered to serve as buglers and drummer boys for the South.

The red-brick inn appears much the same as it did in 1863. The front parlor is tastefully decorated with antique period furniture and features a red Oriental rug. Civil War paintings and intricate, old maps adorn the walls, and the original oak floorboards add to the rustic venue's authentic ambiance. You may feel yourself transported back in time.

Next to the sitting room, an entire room is dedicated to a haunting display of photographs taken over the years by patrons and paranormal investigators. These artifacts feature shadowy figures, bright orbs, and mysterious gray mists that form inside the confines of the inn. The phenomena ramps up in July, as the disembodied souls from a senseless and tragic war reach out to the living and struggle to have their voices heard.

Jack Paladino, former owner of the inn, stated: "We've had nine runners (a guest who flees in terror during the night) in my time here. Some of them left their keys dangling in the door." Current owner Jeremy Davis has become a local historian, and he was generous enough to share some of his extensive research with me. He and Danielle have seen shadow figures from time to time, and very often, heard footsteps. They have seen doors unlatch themselves, swing open, and then latch themselves closed again. It happened one night in full view of a group gathered in the tavern in order to enjoy a lecture on the inn's history. Four people saw the latch move, yet nobody had entered the building. On another night, Jeremy heard a loud thump on the second-floor landing. He ran up the stairs and found a hardcover book standing upright in the center of the floor. The title was *Tales from the Grave*. Apparently, some of their ghosts have a sense of humor.

A few guests have reported encountering the specter of a woman wearing a white dress. Danielle feels that the spirit fits the description of Jacob Mickley's daughter, who would have been living there when the Confederate troops occupied the inn. Very often, pennies will appear out of thin air. Danielle heard one fall to the floor only moments after she had finished vacuuming. Three employees working in the kitchen at night heard the sound of silverware bouncing off of the stove. They realized that a fork had been flung from one of the kitchen tables.

Their various spirits are not confined to the inn. One evening, as Jeremy returned home from a trip to the store, he saw a young soldier in a gray Civil War uniform, carrying a knapsack and a musket, and walking directly towards his oncoming truck. Jeremy swerved and applied the brakes, but it was too late. He watched in shock as the figure passed right through the truck, glancing his way and looking him right in the eye as the vehicle came to a screeching stop. Jeremy jumped out and examined the road. There was no sign of any soldier. A few years later, on a cold and rainy September night, he had been backing his truck out of a parking lot. Jeremy turned his head to check the oncoming traffic, and when he looked forward again, a translucent figure walked across his path, passed right through a wooden fence, and then vanished.

The couple own a second property roughly half a mile up the road. As they were looking into purchasing the home, they noticed that the grass surrounding it had faded to brown, no flowers bloomed, and many of the trees appeared to be stunted. Their real estate agent told them that the place always had an unsettling feeling, so they called in a local psychic. She pulled her car into the driveway, sat there for ten minutes, then told them, "This has something to do with Native American spirits. I don't have enough energy to deal with it," and she left. A second medium told them the same thing; the

The inn has been operating since 1815. The original proprietor, Peter Marck, only accepted cash in advance.

place had an oppressive energy field, and it was somehow related to the Indigenous tribe that once called it home.

Jeremy still did not believe the building had been cursed with bad karma, so the couple went ahead and purchased the property. From time to time, they both heard strange noises late in the night, pounding footsteps, and whispered voices, so Jeremy began to research the history of the site. He found there had been a Lenape village located there in the late 1600s. A raiding party made of Seneca warriors descended upon them by cover of night and burned down the entire village, killing children and braves alike, assaulting the women and taking the rest as slaves, who were then sold to western tribes. Bad karma, indeed. Jeremy was becoming a believer.

Weeks later, Jeremy and Danielle had been crossing the street with their young daughter, when she suddenly cried out in pain. Jeremy examined her foot and discovered a hole in the sole of her shoe and a gushing wound on the bottom of her foot. They carefully searched the road but could find nothing that could puncture a shoe.

Furious, and determined that this aggression had to end, he stormed into the building, stood in the living room, and spoke directly to the Indigenous spirits, telling them that he understood their pain, and he would let every person he encountered know what had happened there. However, if they attacked his family again, he would return there after his own death and give them a war they would soon regret. In the weeks and months afterward, the flowers returned, and verdant grass began to grow. Since that point, there has been no more paranormal activity.

Jeremy led me down into the cellar of the Cashtown Inn and pointed out the window where amputated limbs had been tossed out into the yard. In 1863, there were three other makeshift hospitals within a mile of the Cashtown Inn. Two red-brick ovens stood in the eastern corner. They once served to feed General Hill's troops; now they are barely visible and crumbling with age. A sump pump worked continuously to remove standing water. Jeremy described how, during the battle, the blood ran so thick that it seeped into the groundwater, turning it a ghastly pink for four days.

The Cashtown Inn has made an appearance on several paranormal TV shows, including an episode on *Ghost Hunters* entitled "The Fear Cage." Renowned actor Sam Elliott stayed in the Robert E. Lee Suite while filming the movie *Gettysburg*. The third-floor suite is their most popular room and features the original, oaken beams beneath a tin roof. A hidden passageway connects two bedrooms on the third floor, and it was here that innkeeper Mary Mickley tried to hide with her family when the Confederate troops first invaded Cashtown.

None of the spirits at the Cashtown Inn have caused any real trouble. They are mostly playful or just looking for attention. If you get a chance to stay at the inn, you will be less than 8 miles from Gettysburg, and you will find a charming, rustic venue hosted by the warm and welcoming Davis family. Take a moment to read through the diaries that are placed in each room for the sole purpose of documenting paranormal activity. You may even get to contribute your own ghost story.

The Cashtown Inn is decorated with antique furniture, Civil War paintings, and vintage photographs.

2

Little Round Top

We know not what mystic power may be possessed by those who are now bivouacking with the dead. I only know the effect, but I dare not explain or deny the cause. Who shall say that Washington was not among the number of those who aided the country he founded.

Col. Joshua Chamberlain
Division Commander at Little Round Top

Did he actually mention George Washington, our first and most famous president, a man who had died almost seventy years earlier? The quote was recorded in 1864 as part of an investigation of alleged paranormal phenomena at Gettysburg, ordered by Edwin Stanton, President Lincoln's secretary of war. Apparently, spirits were walking the fields at Gettysburg even before the battle began. Several Union soldiers had described an appearance by the ghost of George Washington as they marched toward the pivotal battle at Little Round Top. Stanton interviewed Union army survivors, and here is the tale he pieced together.

Under the command of Colonel Joshua Chamberlain, the 20th Maine Division were marching north towards Gettysburg when they encountered a fork in the road that had not been noted on their maps. They paused to discuss the decision when a mounted horseman came trotting out of the woods and placed himself at the head of the column. He did not wear a Union uniform, and his style of clothing appeared about fifty years out of date. Most of the men had seen paintings of President Washington and they swore he bore a startling resemblance to this mysterious rider. With an air of supreme confidence, the horseman assured Colonel Chamberlain that he knew the way to their destination, and they soon fell in line behind him. Sure enough, he led them to Gettysburg.

It was early evening by the time they reached the hillside at Little Round Top, and as the waning sun began to set, they noticed an eerie glow emanating from their mysterious guide. The rider had not spoken a single word since he had taken the lead, and before Colonel Chamberlain had a chance to speak with him again, the man turned and rode off into the forest. The troops were convinced that it had been General Washington's spirit who guided them to that pivotal point in history. Perhaps the father of our country inspired his Federal soldiers to fight so courageously on that hilltop, and that was enough to turn the tide of battle.

A majestic statue of Union General Kemble Warren towers over Little Round Top and the Valley of Death.

The landscape at Little Round Top has changed very little since the Battle of Gettysburg. (*Photograph by Mathew Brady, 1863*)

Little Round Top rises to the south of Gettysburg. It is a granite outcropping offering a commanding view of the battlefield below, and a secure ridge on which to mount a defense. Confederate troops conducted an unsuccessful assault on the hill on July 2, 1863. When the battle ended, the Union had lost 139 soldiers, but they had killed or mortally wounded 279 Confederate troops.

Brigadier General Evander Law led the Confederate charge, having marched his soldiers almost 20 miles in order to attack the hillside before the Union army could receive reinforcements. But the July heat had taken its toll, and his exhausted troops never took the time to locate water and fill their depleted canteens. General Law ordered the 4th, 15th, and 47th Alabama Brigades to join the 4th and 5th Texas Brigades and take the hill.

Colonel Strong Vincent commanded the Union brigade. He was wounded early in the battle and died only five days later. His men repelled the first assault with an aggressive volley, forcing the Confederates to withdraw and regroup. The rebels positioned the 15th Alabama Brigade to the right side of the hill, hoping to separate the Union's left flank.

The Union left flank, commanded brilliantly by Joshua Chamberlain, consisted of 386 men of the 20th Maine Regiment and the 83rd Pennsylvania. Recognizing the strategy, Chamberlain stretched his line out to form a single file during the skirmish, then ordered half of them to swing back when the fighting abated. They then formed an angle to the main line which prevented the Confederates from breaking through their left flank.

Chamberlain later stated, "Desperate as the chances were, there was nothing for it but to take the offensive." His soldiers were low on ammunition, and Chamberlain knew they could not survive another assault. He ordered the men to equip bayonets and charge. As the first line engaged in hand-to-hand fighting, the second line charged forward with a fierce battle cry, and the Confederate line broke. Lt. Holman Melcher ordered his unit to charge from the center of the hill and the Confederate regiment retreated in disarray. Company B from the Union's 20th Maine Regiment emerged from the left side and struck the rebels with a devastating volley. The Union division held the hill. There were short skirmishes for the remainder of the day, but the Confederate troops had been defeated. In later years, Chamberlain received a Medal of Honor for his tenacious defense at Little Round Top. The battle for control of the ridge is considered a pivotal turning point at Gettysburg. Theodor Gerrish, a survivor at Little Round Top, wrote: "The rebels were confounded at the movement. We struck them with a fearful shock. They recoil, stagger, break and run, and like avenging demons our men pursue."

There are two other ghost stories that took place at Little Round Top, both involving Civil War reenactors.

Released in 1993, the movie *Gettysburg* was a riveting depiction of the battle that took place in July 1863. As you can imagine, a production like that will employ thousands of extras, many of them professional reenactors who supply their own weaponry and wardrobe. Civil War reenactors take their hobby very seriously, and they are extremely careful to accurately reproduce the uniforms, armament, and conditions of the time period, right down to the meals that the Union soldiers were supplied. In between filming the battle scenes, the actors had plenty of time to explore the battlefield, National Park, and historic sites. The studio filmed in July, hoping to reproduce the conditions in 1863 as accurately as possible.

One sultry evening, just at dusk, four of the actors decided to view the field from the rocky peak at Little Round Top. They hiked up the peaceful hillside, settled at the top, sat around talking for a while and enjoying the sunset, when one of them noticed another

The Union's left flank on the slope of Little Round Top was bravely defended by Colonel Joshua Chamberlain and the 20th Maine Division.

soldier emerge from the tree line. Somewhat filthy and haggard, the old warrior waved to them and climbed up the hillside. As he came closer, they marveled at the accuracy he had managed to achieve. He smelled of sulfur, his beard was unkempt, his boots were torn, and his uniform indicated that he was a Union private. There were powder marks around his mouth, as if he had bitten into his powder cartridge every time he loaded his musket, an impressive detail, even by their high standards. In a Northern accent, he said, "Tough one today, eh boys?" Then, he reached into his powder box, handed them a few rounds of ammunition and added, "Take these, boys. You may need 'em tomorrow." He turned and walked back down the hillside, disappearing into the gathering mist.

The actors carefully examined the rounds, noting how much work it must have taken to reproduce them so well. They were obviously different from the fakes supplied to them for filming. They showed them to the specialist in charge of weaponry, who confirmed their assessment; they were too authentic to be part of the movie crew's production. For the sake of safety, actors are not allowed to use ramrods or live rounds.

The next day they found an antiques dealer in Gettysburg. He confirmed that the rounds were more than 150 years old and offered to buy them. A chill ran down their spines. That old soldier they encountered may have appeared as solid as one of them, but they now realized he was a phantom who had somehow slipped between the boundaries of space and time. They had spoken with a man who died on the battlefield and was very likely buried where he had fallen.

In 1987, a group of foreign dignitaries were hosted in Gettysburg by the United States National Park Service. The park rangers usually served as their guides, showing

Plum Run was said to have turned red with the blood of fallen soldiers.

them all the highlights of the battlefield and explaining the significance of each battle. Oftentimes, they explored the park on their own. At one point, they hiked up the slope of Little Round Top and were greatly impressed by the view. From the crest of the hill, they could see Devil's Den, the Valley of Death, and the site of Pickett's Charge, among others. It was late morning in October. As they sat atop the hill, they witnessed an entire Union army division march into view, their shining muskets slung over their shoulders in perfect alignment. As their commander shouted orders, the men turned in unison, as a well-trained army is expected to do. The visitors commented to each other on the accuracy of the uniforms; the incredible precision performed by what they had assumed were Civil War reenactors. The Union soldiers went through a series of maneuvers, then turned as one and marched quickly out of sight.

The dignitaries eventually sauntered back to the headquarters for the National Park and were eager to express their appreciation for that special and unexpected demonstration. The park rangers had no idea what they were talking about. They checked their schedules and found no indication that reenactors would be using the field that day. There is a very formal process for getting permission, and it is virtually impossible for a group to sneak into the park without their knowledge. Besides, nobody else had seen them marching. The dignitaries had all heard the ghost stories about "the Phantom Regiment" at Gettysburg. Now, they had one of their own.

Sturdy breastworks constructed at the summit of the hill served to repel Confederate attacks. (*Photograph by Alexander Gardner, July 1863*)

One of the more prevalent theories regarding the existence of ghosts involves time and how it is perceived. Theoretical physicists have posited that events in time may not actually occur in sequence; that is just how we perceive and measure them. It is possible that events are constantly happening everywhere, and all at once. With this in mind, it may be possible to experience an overlap in time periods, a sort of brief window into the past. Often called a "Time Slip," the phenomenon may occur naturally, or may be the result of certain conditions that align every 300 days, or 500 years. The men and women who witnessed the marching soldiers may not have seen a ghost at all; they may have been peering 125 years into the past. It is conceivable that the witnesses themselves may have stepped into one of these temporal overlaps, and for ten or twenty minutes, may have journeyed into the past. Phenomena such as these have been reported countless times and in many locations around the world. Perhaps Gettysburg is one such occurrence, where the tragic events that took place in America's Civil War have somehow affected the flow of time, causing the scenes of the distant past to overlap with the present. It is a plausible theory that may explain the incredible variety of ghost sightings and paranormal phenomena reported in this one area.

The western slope of Little Round Top was the scene of intense fighting. It later became known as "the Slaughter Pen."

3

Sachs Covered Bridge

To the south of Gettysburg, the Sachs Covered Bridge, which spans Marsh Creek, lies between the townships of Cumberland and Freedom. If you plan to visit, drive south on Waterworks Road and you will find it just past the Eisenhower Estate.

Originally constructed in 1852 by David Stoner, Sachs is a town-truss bridge, a design based on the patent issued to Ithiel Town in 1820. Instead of heavy piers, the supporting frame was constructed with wooden beams, plank floors, and detailed lattice work. Both Union and Confederate troops crossed it before and after the Battle of Gettysburg, and its proximity to the flowing water of Marsh Creek enabled the rebel troops to set up temporary field hospitals along the riverbank. This might have contributed to the bridge's haunted reputation, as more than half of the wounded men held in triage died in agony from devastating wounds or rampant infection, some with their limbs amputated.

General Lee's troops crossed Sachs Covered Bridge both before and after the battle.

The bridge is an engineering marvel, and only a few of its kind remain in Pennsylvania. It somehow survived a flash flood in 1996 that destroyed three other steel bridges, although major portions of Sachs Bridge were dislodged and washed downstream. Once the floods abated, the intact sections were reunited, and the bridge was completely renovated with steel support beams. The bridge is structurally sound but is now limited to foot traffic due to its historical significance.

Even by Gettysburg standards, the bridge is considered a true paranormal hotspot. Sachs Bridge is guaranteed to provide you some form of otherworldly phenomenon, especially if you visit late at night. Stroll across its 150-foot length in the silvery moonlight and you may hear gunshots, galloping horses, or cannon fire. Linger for a while longer and you may hear a disembodied voice, see a floating orb, or a dark mist that forms a vaguely humanoid shape, you may smell sulfur or tobacco, hear phantom footsteps following behind you, or be overcome with intense feelings of fear or sadness. Some visitors even claim to have seen the spectral image of General Robert E. Lee, smoking a pipe and leaning against the rail, guiding his demoralized troops as they retreated to the South. But the most frightening apparition of all is the ghastly specter of three human bodies dangling from the wooden beams that form the bridge's rooftop. Sometimes they take the form of disembodied heads suspended above many a horrified visitor, or drifting along the side of the railing before disappearing into the river's shrouded mist.

According to local folklore, the hauntings are linked to the execution of three Federal soldiers. During their march towards the upcoming battle at Gettysburg, the Union army caught three deserters and made an example of them. They were hung from

Late at night, the historic bridge casts an oppressive pall over those who venture into its embrace.

the wooden support beams, their rotting corpses left there for days in full display as a warning to the other soldiers. Some variations claim that the captives were rebel spies, others describe them as Confederate deserters who tried to pass themselves off as Federal soldiers. Whatever the true version of events, there is no doubt that their tormented spirits have chosen to remain where they were brutally executed. The bridge is most certainly haunted.

Gettysburg police and firefighters are often called to the site by frantic reports of a raging fire that threatens to consume the historic structure. When they arrive in force with sirens wailing, they seldom find any sign of smoke or fire. However, many of the firefighters admitted to seeing a bright, red glow that suddenly winks out as they approach. There is just an incredible variety of phenomena associated with Sachs Covered Bridge.

After three days of heavy fighting, General Lee had lost the battle and was forced to retreat, burdened by the need to ferry hundreds of his wounded soldiers back to Maryland and Virginia. Heavy rains were falling on July 4. Most of the wounded Confederates were loaded onto spring-less wagons for a long and torturous journey over uneven ground. Civil War veterans recalled that Sachs bridge was literally soaked in the seeping blood of the rebel troops. It is easy to imagine this horrific scene and understand how the bridge might be infused with this intense trauma.

A spirit given the nickname "Tennessee" has been known to interact with visitors. Tennessee is believed to be an escaped slave, and he seems particularly fond of cigarettes. If you leave an offering of tobacco for him, you may entice him to interact with you. Countless ghost hunters have tried this technique, with varying success.

Several field hospitals were employed along the shores of Marsh Creek.

Sarah Jones (fictional name) arrived at the bridge on a cold November evening in 2014. She had purchased a pack of cigarettes for the occasion. She and her friend, Bill, parked at the southern end of the bridge and walked along its 150-foot length, pausing in the middle to conduct an experiment. Sarah had to admit the place had an eerie vibe to it. She later described the sensation as "unsettling." Sarah opened the small pack and lit one of the cigarettes. She inhaled a puff of smoke and then placed it on the rail, careful to stand between the light breeze and the cigarette. Then, she asked Tennessee if he would like to smoke it with her. Minutes went by, and their eyes remained locked on the cigarette, its burning tip glowing bright red in the darkness. Suddenly, she saw it move. Sarah practically jumped out of her skin but quickly regained her composure. Addressing the spirit, she said, "I brought you an offering. I'd like to think it was you who moved that cigarette. Can you do it again?" They saw no further movement for ten minutes. They were just about to give up when the cigarette stirred, and this time the ember glowed more brightly, as if some unseen specter had inhaled the smoke. "Did you see that?" she shouted to Bill. Bill's eyes were popping out of his head, but he managed to reply, "I sure did! I think he took a drag!"

Hearing a ghost story is one thing; seeing it play out while you are standing in the pale moonlight on a haunted bridge is something else entirely. I have seen experienced ghost hunters freeze up when something truly paranormal happens. Sarah felt panic rising. She grabbed Bill's arm and shouted, "I need to leave!"

Bill started to follow Sarah but then he turned back and said, "When you're done smoking it, can you do something for us? Can you push it over the edge?" Another two minutes passed before they saw it move again. For the second time, the embers glowed more brightly. "That's it!" said Sarah. "I'm leaving." She turned to go but could not resist taking one last look at the cigarette. It was gone. Either the winter breeze had caught it, or the mischievous ghost of Tennessee had pushed it off the rail. They quickened their pace and scurried off the bridge, grateful when they reached the relative safety of the car. Once they had the engine running, Bill said, "I saw what happened. That wasn't caused by the wind. Your ghost flicked that cigarette off the rail!"

Sachs Covered Bridge may be a picturesque spot by the light of day but take a quiet stroll across it under the shroud of darkness and you might encounter a gruesome scene from the distant past. In the same manner that it spans Marsh Creek, perhaps the iconic bridge serves as a conduit between the world of the living and that of the dead.

Visitors describe the horrifying sight of three soldiers who had been executed, swinging from the rafters above Sachs Bridge.

Phantom voices call out from the shrouded mists below the bridge.

4

THE TILLIE PIERCE HOUSE INN

In July 1863, Matilda "Tillie" Pierce was a young girl of fifteen attending the Young Ladies Seminary, a private finishing school on West High Street in the sleepy, little town of Gettysburg. Within days, all Hell broke loose, and she found herself at the center of a pivotal battle that would soon determine the fate of the Union.

For weeks, the town had heard rumors that the rebel army was approaching Gettysburg. Only days earlier, General Lee had reached Chambersburg in nearby Franklin County. Confederate troops arrived in late June 1863. Tillie and her sister, Maggie, attended school on the morning of June 28. Hours later, rebel soldiers were spotted on the outskirts of town, their classes were immediately canceled, and the girls hurried home to help the Pierce family fortify their home and possessions. Southern infantrymen were already raiding the town's food stores and commandeering horses for their upcoming stand against the Army of the Potomac. The family barricaded their doors and felt safe for the time being, as the rebels moved along towards Seminary Ridge, where they would soon engage a Union brigade commanded by General Rufus Dawes. Dawes was the great-grandson of William Dawes, the second rider sent out with Paul Revere on his midnight ride to warn the Minutemen. Two days later, the entire Union army arrived under General George Meade.

Both of Tillie's older brothers had already signed up to defend the North, so the girls felt a surge of pride as the blue-clad soldiers of Buford's Cavalry, almost 6,000 strong, entered Gettysburg and marched north on Washington Street. Stationing themselves on a visible corner with a group of friends, they sang out "Our Union Forever" seeking to encourage the men, and marveling that so many of them appeared younger than Tillie. She then got her first taste of the true horrors of war, as wagon after wagon filled with wounded and bandaged soldiers, some of them on stretchers and already missing eyes, hands, and legs, trudged along behind the cavalry.

That evening, Tillie's parents decided to send both girls southward, to a farmhouse owned by their friend Jacob Weikert, which, unfortunately, was located at the foot of a rocky hill called Little Round Top. The ridge turned out to be a strategic point of contention in the ensuing conflict, and for the next three days the battle intensified, placing the girls in great danger. On July 1, the farmhouse was converted to a military field hospital, and the Weikerts' two-story home now served as General Meade's headquarters.

Young Tillie had to grow up quickly. She witnessed incredible suffering, as a procession of wounded Union soldiers were carried into the farmhouse on stretchers. Some might

The Tillie Pierce Inn has operated since 1829.

have wilted, but Tillie was not one of them. She jumped right in to assist, at first supplying buckets of water, then baking bread or making soup, but eventually bandaging wounds and comforting the young men as they died in her arms or endured painful amputations.

Tillie would survive the battle and go on to write a book about her terrifying experience, *At Gettysburg, or What a Girl Saw and Heard of the Battle: A True Narrative* (apparently brevity had not yet come into style). In her own words, she described the scene: "Some limping, some with their heads and arms in bandages, some crawling, others carried on stretchers or brought in ambulances. Suffering, cast down and dejected, it was a truly pitiable gathering. Before night the barn was filled with the shattered and dying heroes of this day's struggle." She later added: "Nothing before in my experience had ever paralleled the sight we then and there beheld. There were the groaning and crying, the struggling and dying, crowded side by side, while attendants sought to aid and relieve them as best they could."

The battle went on for three days. When the dust had settled, the fields were covered with bodies, and it was the townsfolk of Gettysburg who were left the grim task of burying hundreds of decomposing rebel corpses. Four days later, Tillie and her sisters returned to their home. She could barely recognize the area. Minie balls and cannister shells had damaged several residential buildings. In her book, she stated how fortunate she had been to survive such a harrowing experience: "The whole landscape had been changed, and I felt as though we were in a strange and blighted land." By some act of divine providence, only one civilian had been killed at Gettysburg, a twenty-year-old named Jenny Wade.

Booted footsteps often reverberate above the second-floor bedrooms, where rebel sharpshooters once took aim at the Federal troops on Cemetery Hill.

Tillie went on to marry Civil War veteran Horace Allemen in 1871, and they raised three children. The couple moved to Selinsgrove, Pennsylvania, in 1890, where Tillie wrote and published her memoir. She passed away in 1914, at the age of sixty-seven.

The Tillie Pierce Inn, a bed and breakfast constructed in 1829, is a two-story, red-brick building topped by a single garret window. The backyard encloses a Victorian-era garden. The interior features a charming dining room, a cozy living room, a large common area, and six bedrooms, all tastefully decorated with nineteenth-century antiques. Most of the larger rooms on the second floor have their own fireplaces. The rooms are color-themed and named for historic figures who assisted during the battle.

I spent a single night at the inn and slept in the Tillie Pierce Room. I tried for hours to record some ghostly voices, then gave up, set up my cameras and went to bed. The camcorders filmed in infrared for seven hours but failed to capture any substantial evidence of a spirit. It was a peaceful night, but at 1:20 a.m., I did feel something pull one of my blankets off the corner of the bed. Immediately, I turned the recorders back on and spoke to the ghosts, but they were not in the mood to communicate. It took me a while to get back to sleep. In the morning, I chatted with the caretaker, Mark, and he relayed a few tales from his own experience. Staff on the second floor have gotten used to hearing booted footsteps in the attic above them. A Confederate sniper had been stationed there during the battle and was very likely killed by a Union sharpshooter. Visitors are often awakened by the departed rebel's shuffling activity, as he relives the final moments of his young life.

Mark had only been working at the inn for a short time, but he resided in Gettysburg. Early one morning, while driving through the National Park, he spied a small group of

Nineteenth-century antiques adorn the living room and common areas.

rebel soldiers crossing the road near the "Bloody Wheatfield." He turned his head to monitor the oncoming traffic and when he looked back, they had completely vanished.

Guests and visitors have heard disembodied voices calling out in the darkness of night, phantom footsteps on the stairway, and loud knocking on their hotel room doors. Others have seen shadowy figures that dance across the walls of their room, felt a light tap on their shoulder, or a sudden drop in temperature on a hot summer night. The old inn also has a ghostly cat. On the second-floor landing, I discovered a collection of cat toys, which guests are encouraged to bring into their rooms for the spirit cat. In the morning light, the toys are sometimes found scattered around the floor.

The phantom specter of a very young woman is often encountered at the inn. Believed to be the ghost of Tillie Pierce, she is usually seen gazing out one of the second-floor windows, she does not interact with visitors and is most often wearing a white dress.

The full-bodied apparition of a young soldier wearing the blue uniform of the Union army has shown himself several times, and this spirit appears to be aware of the other guests. Visitors describe him wearing a confused expression, some have said he raises his arm to attract their attention, and others report that he sits on the edge of their beds and stares blankly at the wall. There is little doubt the young man was killed at Gettysburg, but what is it that keeps him rooted to the inn? Is he unaware that he has died, or is the figure merely an echo of a living soul, an energetic impression somehow burned into the fabric of the inn by the violent nature of his death? Perhaps there exists some unexplained phenomenon at the Tillie Pierce Inn which presents visitors a window into the past for one brief moment, a glimpse of the horrors perpetrated on the field of battle, more than 160 years ago.

The Blue Room is considered the most active area at the Tillie Pierce Inn.

Young Tillie was only fifteen when she found herself pressed into service assisting Union army surgeons.

5

KUHN'S BRICKYARD

The battle for Kuhn's Brickyard took place on July 1 and was one of the earliest skirmishes in the three-day conflict. Only portions of the two armies took part, whereas by day three, the bulk of both armies were involved in the struggle to control Gettysburg. The brickyard fight has largely been treated as a footnote when compared to the expansive campaigns that took place at Little Round Top, the Slaughter Pen, and the Valley of Death. But it may have served the Army of the Potomac well by slowing down the Confederate advance toward Cemetery Hill.

At the center of the brickyard stands a monument dedicated to the 154th New York Infantry.

The brickyard skirmish was a complete route in favor of the Confederate Army, as they arrived with two full brigades and significantly outnumbered the Union force commanded by Colonel Charles Coster. Coster's three small regiments had been sent from Cemetery Hill to buy some time as the Eleventh Core retreated ahead of a superior Confederate force surging into Gettysburg. Coster's unit had been further weakened when fifty of his men were sent to reconnaissance at Sabillasville, leaving him with 1,260 troops. Coster's soldiers sheltered behind a brickyard fence. Their vision may have been obscured by the tall grass growing in the wheat field, allowing the rebels to approach within 200 yards before being spotted.

Two Confederate brigades under General Harry Hayes and Colonel Isaac Avery descended upon Coster's unit much too quickly for the Union soldiers to defend and, although shots were fired, the battle soon turned into hand-to-hand fighting. Completely overwhelmed, the Union line broke and most of Coster's brave men were killed or captured. The survivors retreated towards Gettysburg, finally joining with the Federal soldiers holding the ridge at Cemetery Hill. Coster had lost 563 of his men, while the Confederates lost only 200.

John Kuhn's brickyard was situated northeast of Gettysburg, and comprised of Kuhn's two-story brick home and backyard, enclosed by wire fences for containing livestock. Behind the house, Kuhn owned an additional acre of land, most of it dedicated to growing wheat. A carriage gateway led from the house to the brickworks,

The brickyard mural was designed and illustrated by historian Mark H. Denkelman, a descendant of a Civil War soldier.

and to a clay mill used for making pottery, bricks, and cement. Behind the mill were four dome-shaped brick kilns. A bubbling stream called Steven's Run ran through the southeastern portion of Kuhn's farmland.

The area that Harrisburg Community College now occupies is adjacent to Kuhn's Brickyard. It was once part of the North Gettysburg Shopping Center, which included a Radio Shack. In the 1970s, their employees often complained that the electronics would turn themselves on and off at random intervals. It was not uncommon for the daytime manager to open the store in the morning and find two or three televisions already turned on, blaring out the news. One Radio Shack employee described the ghostly image of a man's face appearing on a TV screen. He turned off the television and watched as the screen slowly faded to black. Then with a shock, he realized that the set had been unplugged!

Rock Creek meanders its way behind this area. There are many theories positing that running water creates energy, and spirits can use that energy to enhance their presence. Writer and historian Mark Nesbitt described his own experience as he conducted some late-night recordings near the creek. When Mark played back the audio, the ghostly voices sounded like they were shouting at him. He politely asked them to stop yelling. A few minutes later, Mark captured an EVP that whispered, "We'll be quiet." Other paranormal groups have captured soldiers' voices on audio, and filmed glowing orbs, hovering at the site of the mural.

The heart-breaking photograph of Sergeant Amos Humiston's three children was featured in news accounts after the battle.

The impressive mural on Coster Avenue was designed and painted by artist and historian Mark H. Denkelman, a descendant of a Civil War survivor. He was assisted by muralist Johan Njurman. At 100 feet wide and 20 feet high, it covers the entire rear wall of the building. The brilliant scene depicts the battle between the two forces, and it also displays the home of John Kuhn, which was struck by a Union cannister shell, still embedded in the brick exterior.

Civil War statistics put the death toll at 625,000 soldiers, almost 2 percent of the United States population. They tell a tragic story, but they are sweeping descriptions of an extended and punishing war. Very often, a more personal tale can pull at the heartstrings with a more lasting effect than the movement of troops or strategic analysis.

One such incident stood out among the carnage at Gettysburg. A Union soldier revealed his last, dying thoughts as he bled out onto the killing fields at Kuhn's Brickyard. When gravediggers and townsfolk began the grim task of identifying and preparing the bodies for burial, hundreds of the decaying corpses had been badly mangled, and carried no form of identification.

One Federal soldier was found at the brickyard, clutching an ambrotype photograph of his three orphaned children. Somehow, the story quickly traveled from mouth to mouth, until it became a national obsession, the heart-wrenching photo eventually featured in newspaper accounts in the hope that some reader could identify the three

John Kuhn's home was struck by a Union cannister shell during the battle. It remains embedded within the brick exterior.

children. Finally, a news article reached the eyes of his young widow in New York, Philinda Humiston. Instantly, she recognized the tin photograph she had given her young soldier to carry with him into battle. Now that the identity of Sergeant Amos Humiston had been revealed to the nation, the plight of his three children, Franklin, Alice, and Frederick—and by extension, thousands of other fatherless families—was brought to light.

It was Dr. John F. Bourns who had examined the corpse and discovered the tin photograph, and he led the charge to assist the children of Sergeant Humiston. According to census bureau data, the number of children living in orphanages after the war increased from 7,700 to an incredible 60,000. Dr. Bourns decided to open an orphanage at the site of battle. In the spring of 1866, the federal government purchased a two-story building and an acre of land from Gettysburg farmer George Wolff and established the National Soldiers' Orphans Homestead, with Dr. Bourns as the administrator. Sergeant Humiston's widow, Philinda, was hired as their first headmistress. The orphanage thrived under Philinda's guidance, but she later remarried and left her position. It was eventually closed down in 1877.

Late at night, phantom voices call out to visitors in the haunted brickyard.

6

THE ROSE FARM

The story of the Rose Farm is a tragedy that extends well beyond the horrific battle at Gettysburg, and an example of the far-reaching repercussions of the Civil War. The country had been torn asunder, and it took many years for it to achieve any semblance of a unified nation.

In 1863, the 2,450 residents of Gettysburg lived barely 10 miles from the Mason–Dixon line, and as dire reports of Confederate conquests inched closer to their doorstep, they knew that their homes and farmland were in danger of being caught between two opposing forces, ransacked for supplies, or damaged beyond repair. For the Rose family, it turned out to be all three.

The Rose farmhouse was continually hit by minie balls and cannister shells.

In 1858, George Rose had been the owner of a profitable, butcher shop in Germantown, Pennsylvania. Born in Philadelphia, he was a true American, a self-made man who was just beginning to enjoy the financial benefits of his many years of hard work. He and his young bride, Dorothea, purchased a rustic stone house that sat on 230 acres of workable farmland in the picturesque town of Gettysburg. Instead of moving into the home, George worked out a deal to lease the farm to his younger brother, John. John Rose, his wife, Ann, and their seven children worked the Rose farm for five years, splitting the profits equally with George, maintaining the two-story home, and hiring additional farmhands during the growing season. In addition, George rented rooms to the Ogden family, so there were ten to twelve people living at the Rose Farm.

It was common knowledge that twenty-three-year-old Charles Francis Ogden and twenty-year-old Mary Josephine Rose had become an item. They were the right age for marriage, and despite the fact that they shared a homestead in common, they had fallen in love. When the Civil War broke out, Charles left home to join the Union army, eventually serving in the 138th Pennsylvania Regiment. As cruel fate would have it, he was sent into battle on that summer morning within 400 yards of his childhood home.

Francis Ogden took his family and a portion of his livestock and moved them to another farm located north of the Susquehanna River, but the rest of the Rose family remained at the farm. On the first day of battle, Confederate troops took control of the stone house and converted it into a field hospital. Young Rose bore witness to the high cost of war, as wounded rebel soldiers were carried into her home in stretchers, filling every room, some screaming in pain, others bleeding out in the Rose family beds, and dying in droves.

As she watched young men suffer and Confederate surgeons perform their gruesome amputations, she knew that Charles was out there in the trenches, fighting for his life, or perhaps he already lay dead on some blood-soaked field. During all three days of the Gettysburg campaign, the Rose farm saw intense fighting, as the two sides battled for control of the wheat field. Author and historian Tim Smith later described the scene as "the bloodiest farm in America."

On July 1, the Confederate Army under Buford's Cavalry occupied the farmland. On the second day, McLaw's Division of Longstreet's Corps battled with the Union 3rd and 5th Corps. On day three, General Kershaw's South Carolina Brigade and General Anderson's Georgia Brigade engaged with the Union's 3rd and 5th Corps. The Union artillery under Colonel McGilvery inflicted severe damage on both the Confederate troops and the Rose farmhouse. The stone building was struck many times by cannister shells and minie balls. Rebel soldiers who survived the gruesome battle described the strange sound of the family dinner bell ringing throughout the day, as errant shots from both armies peppered the Rose family home, smashing windows and tearing gaping holes in the stone facade. The Rose's once peaceful farmland later became known as "the Bloody Wheatfield," the hard-fought terrain changing hands six times in three days.

When the battle finally ended and the Confederate troops had withdrawn, the fallen bodies of both armies literally covered the Wheatfield. Over the next five days, Union soldiers buried them where they had fallen, in shallow and unmarked gravesites. This brutal task took many days to complete, with the corpses gradually decomposing in the stifling summer heat.

The famous images captured by photographer Alexander Gardner displayed bloodied corpses in various stages of decay, some of them propped up against trees, others tossed into hastily dug trenches, their bloated faces staring up at the uncaring summer

Some of the most intense fighting took place in the Wheatfield and Peach Orchard, both situated on the Rose family property.

sky. Government estimates determined that 400–500 bodies were interred across the Wheatfield, and some in the front yard of the Rose farmhouse. In November 1863, the Union army began the daunting task of exhuming the dead and moving them to consecrated ground, but this grim chore took almost five more years.

Mary Rose received word that Charles Ogden had survived the battle. Only three days later, her fragile hopes were once again crushed. Charles had been killed in a skirmish further to the south. One can only imagine what went through her young mind, as she pictured her beloved soldier buried like a wild dog in some other mass gravesite, with not even a wooden marker to let the world know where he had fallen. It was too much for the poor woman. In the following weeks, her mental health quickly deteriorated. Watching the hundreds of bodies being slowly exhumed seems to have been her breaking point. Rose family survivors say that she began to scream about blood pouring through the walls of their home. Poor Mary was beyond their help, and the family called in the town doctor, J. W. C. O'Neil. Young Mary was taken out in a straitjacket and placed in an insane asylum, where she would spend the rest of her tortured life.

Some believe that Mary has returned to the Rose Farm after death. To this day, visitors to the Wheatfield in early July report hearing the ghastly screams of a woman piercing the summer night. Perhaps Mary Rose is still out there, roaming the fields and forever searching for her beloved Charles.

Mary is not the only specter encountered at the Bloody Wheatfield. Within a few weeks of the Battle of Gettysburg, villagers reported seeing glowing orbs of light floating through the trees beyond the field. In later years, all kinds of phenomena have been experienced; apparitions of both Union and Confederate soldiers, entire regiments marching in formation, men shouting, cannon fire, the sound of horses galloping, and ghostly voices calling out in the night.

The Rose barn, once employed as a field hospital, was badly damaged in the battle.

Becky Lyons, a park ranger for many years at Gettysburg, has collected quite a few ghost stories. One fellow ranger told her that she was driving past the Rose Farm one night and spotted campfires in the Wheatfield. She called it in, believing that some visitors had camped there in defiance of the park rules. The ranger on nighttime duty went out to investigate but found no sign of any fires. In the morning, they inspected the field but there was no evidence of a campsite. Fire and flickering lights are one of the most common phenomena reported in many of the Gettysburg battle sites.

Becky and some fellow historians called in a well-known psychic to get her assessment of the hauntings. Working in a trance state, the woman described quite a few impressions as she walked across the hallowed grounds. She stopped in the center of the Bloody Wheatfield and said that a small but ambitious man, much like Napoleon, had fallen at that spot. It was indeed the very area where the 5-foot 2-inch Colonel Henry Merwin was felled by a rebel sniper. In another area, she stated that two men with the same last name had met their maker within yards of one another. Further research through Union military records turned up Brigadier General Samuel Zook and his brother, Daniel, both listed as casualties during the second day of battle. What discarnate spirits were sending her these tragic details, specific information that she had no way of knowing?

Is it possible that not all the fallen bodies were recovered? Are there missing and forgotten soldiers roaming throughout the night at Gettysburg, longing to have their shattered bones recovered, their earthly remains properly buried on consecrated ground, or merely to be afforded the courtesy of a simple grave marker?

The Bloody Wheatfield will forever contain the permanent record of a brutal slaughterhouse, an event so traumatic that it infused the very soil with its eternal memory.

Only desolate ruins remain where the barn once stood.

Confederate soldiers await burial at the Wheatfield. When the battle had finally ended, the field was littered with bodies. (*Photograph by Timothy O'Sullivan, 1863*)

7

The Devil's Den

The name "Devil's Den" has been given to a small ridge containing a tangled maze of massive boulders and shadowy crevices that lies southwest of Little Round Top. The moniker predates the Civil War and so does its supernatural connection. In Gettysburg folklore, it was believed to have been the sight of a violent battle between Native American tribes known as "the Battle of the Crows." In the darkness of the Gettysburg night, Indigenous war cries and percussive drumbeats have echoed throughout the granite outcropping, as far back as the 1700s. Supposedly, the Den was once infested with snakes, but it is more than likely that the area derives its name from the sharp crevices that are cut into the cliff side, their shadows so deep and dark that they give the impression that the clefts extend all the way down into Lucifer's domain.

The summit of Little Round Top overlooks Devil's Den, Plum Run, and the Slaughter Pen.

On the second day of the Battle of Gettysburg, the ridge became the epicenter of the fight, with both armies taking control of Devil's Den and then relinquishing it. The bloody outcropping changed hands three times in a single day. General Robert E. Lee sent General James Longstreet to attack the Union's flank at Little Round Top, while General Lafayette McLaws assaulted the Wheatfield, the Peach Orchard, and Devil's Den. Inexplicably, the Union's General Sickles decided to abandon Little Round Top and move his troops forward to the Peach Orchard, which opened both of his flanks. However, the Southern brigades approaching the Wheatfield had been delayed by rough terrain and some confusion in the chain of command. When the battle engaged, it soon dissolved into complete chaos.

The rebels hailing from Alabama, Texas, Arkansas, and Georgia charged across the Wheatfield to assault the Union divisions from New York, Maine, and Pennsylvania. Both sides were frustrated and confused by the scattering of large boulders, and their regiments quickly broke down into smaller units engaged in hand-to-hand combat. Union and Confederate soldiers alike ducked behind the boulders or concealed themselves in the narrow clefts, where they could ambush their enemies with the thrust of a bayonet. Deadly cannon fire from Cemetery Hill continually tore into the rebel fighters, causing so much carnage that the area surrounding the battle became known as "The Slaughter Pen."

The granite outcropping changed hands three times during the furious battle.

The South briefly held the ridge at Devil's Den but were soon overwhelmed by a second swarm of Federal troops. As the bodies began to accumulate among the boulders, the Georgia unit charged once more across the Slaughter Pen and managed to drive the Union troops out of the granite outcropping. Their snipers then nestled into the crevices and used the boulders for shelter while they picked off Federal soldiers on Little Round Top.

As night fell and the shooting abated, the rebels who survived the siege described an eerie scenario, sharing the hard-fought ridge with hundreds of dead and dying men, their cries for help echoing throughout the night. In the area surrounding Devil's Den, 2,600 men had lost their lives in a single day. On the morning of July 4, heavy rains fell, flooding the creek and drowning some of the wounded men still trapped on the field.

Devil's Den is considered one of the most haunted areas at Gettysburg. The Confederate Army had lost 1,800 soldiers in a single day, and almost 800 Union troops had been killed. The sharp sound of gunfire is most often reported, along with the haunting cry of a wounded soldier in the small area between the stream and the ridge. Apparitions of Union and Confederate soldiers walk among the granite boulders or stand at the edge of the ridge, gazing across the Wheatfield. In the Triangular Field above the ridge, cell phones and cameras experience unusual electronic glitches. Photographers often find their batteries drained of power.

Historians speculate that some photographs of fallen soldiers at Devil's Den may have been staged. (*Photograph by Timothy O'Sullivan, 1863. Library of Congress*)

Devil's Den is frequented by a friendly ghost the park rangers have named "the Helpful Hippy." He wears a large floppy hat, torn trousers, and walks barefoot. His face is covered in soot, and his long scraggly hair hangs to his shoulders. Historians speculate that fighters from the Texas Brigade that controlled Devil's Den for a short time fit this description. Many of the men who signed up for the Army of Northern Virginia were never issued full uniforms or consistent armament. Visitors who pause to gaze at their maps or take a photograph have been approached by this specter, whom they assume to be a living person. He usually points to the stream and tells them, "That's what you're looking for." After the battle, the creek named Plum Run became known as "the Bloody Run" because it had literally turned red with the spilled blood of fallen soldiers. It is possible this amicable spirit had been one of the drowning victims, or perhaps his unmarked grave lies in that direction.

But not all the spirits at Devil's Den are quite as friendly. Twenty years ago, a visitor claimed that as she stood atop one of the boulders, she felt a clammy hand clutch at her ankle. She looked down and saw a wounded Confederate soldier wedged inside the crevice, begging for help. Her startled scream brought other visitors running to her side, but the specter had vanished without a trace.

The apparition of a rebel soldier known as "the Helpful Hippy" often appears to startled visitors at Devil's Den.

On July 5, 1863, the blood-soaked fields were still covered with countless bodies in various levels of decay. A professional photographer named Alexander Gardner arrived to document the Battle of Gettysburg, and he took a graphic photograph displaying the body of a rebel sharpshooter lying amongst the boulders at Devil's Den. He later published the image in his 1865 collection *Photographic Sketch Book of the Civil War*. A full century later, an astute historian noticed that the same body showed up in Gardner's photographic archives, this time placed in a different area of the battle. Since Gardner had passed away, it was never determined whether he had moved the body or just staged the shots with a corporeal actor.

Whatever the sinister origins of the name, Devil's Den had set the stage for carnage on a much higher level. The Bloody Wheatfield, the Slaughter Pen, and Devil's Den are among the most haunted areas on the field of battle. It is often theorized that the accumulation of traumatic energy has caused its earth-bound spirits to remain trapped there in some cruel form of limbo, forever replaying the violent battle that took their young lives.

Protected by massive boulders, Confederate snipers could easily pick off Union troops entrenched at the summit of Little Round Top.

There appears to be one or more figures in this intriguing photograph of the Triangular Field. (*Photograph by Lourdes Vicente*)

A rebel sharpshooter spent his last moments at Devil's Den. (*Photograph by Timothy O'Sullivan, 1863*)

8

The Valley of Death

Climb to the peak of Little Round Top and you will be awarded a sweeping view of the battlefield, much as it appeared in 1863. You will be able to pick out a maze of boulders called Devil's Den and a meandering creek named Plum Run. Beyond that lies the Bloody Wheatfield, the Rose Woods, and the Peach Orchard, all of them scenes of violent battles. But the area below the western slope of Little Round Top saw carnage at an entirely different level, rightly earning its gruesome moniker "the Slaughter Pen." By the time the Battle of Gettysburg had ended, every inch of the ground was covered with dead bodies.

On July 1, 1863, General Henry Heth and General A. P. Hill surged into the town of Gettysburg with the bulk of the Army of Northern Virginia and engaged with Federal troops. Heavily outnumbered, the small Union force retreated through the town and regrouped on the high ground at Cemetery Hill. The Union force was now firmly entrenched at the top of Culp's Hill and thinly spread across the ridge at Cemetery Hill, barely holding out while awaiting the arrival of Major General Meade. George Meade and his 90,000 Federal troops arrived late in the evening.

Joshua Chamberlain, having been promoted to colonel of the 20th Maine for his leadership at the Battle of Chancellorsville, received urgent orders to march to Gettysburg. They arrived late in the day and were ordered to ascend to the left flank at Little Round Top and hold it against General Longstreet's Confederate brigades, which were approaching from the west. The rebels hit them with a barrage of heavy artillery as they assaulted the hill. The intense fighting escalated into close-quarter, hand-to-hand combat.

According to the eyewitness of dozens of Union soldiers, the tall horseman who had guided General Meade's army to the scene of the battle on July 1 suddenly reappeared and rode to the front of the line. He wore an old-fashioned uniform and a tricorn hat. The Confederates also spotted the phantom rider, and they fired shot after shot at him, but he never fell.

His troops low on ammunition, Chamberlain feared the battle would be lost. Then, in his own words, "Suddenly, an imposing figure stood in front of the line exhorting them to follow. The rays of the afternoon sun set his upraised sword aflame. The men were filled with hope and bravery. They fixed their bayonets and charged into the line of the Confederates." The rebel line broke and retreated, some of them running down the slope. The Union's 83rd Pennsylvania met them on the hillside and caught them in a deadly

From the summit of Little Round Top, you can view the Slaughter Pen, Devil's Den, the Triangular Field, Plum Run, and the Valley of Death.

When the battle had ended, Confederate bodies littered the ground across the Slaughter Pen. (*Photograph by Taylor & Huntington. Published in War Memories, the War for the Union, 1890*)

crossfire. A total of 400 Confederate soldiers surrendered and were taken prisoner. The mysterious apparition had turned the tide of the crucial battle and perhaps ensured the future of America. Joshua Chamberlain managed to survive the war, and he later went on to be elected governor of Maine. Quoted in his memoirs, he maintained that something unearthly had indeed come to their aid in that pivotal battle at Gettysburg.

On the second day of battle, Union General Dan Sickles moved his troops from the southern edge of Cemetery Ridge west to the Peach Orchard, exposing both of his flanks. Confederate forces overwhelmed them, taking control of the Wheatfield, the Peach Orchard, and Devil's Den. For hours, the two armies engaged in some of the bloodiest combat of the Civil War, both sides taking and then losing control of the contested terrain. More than 8,000 lives were lost in a single day, almost a third of the troops the two armies brought to Gettysburg. This blood-soaked battleground soon became known as "the Valley of Death."

General Richard Ewell attacked the Union positions at Little Round Top, Cemetery Hill, and Culp's Hill, but the Federal troops dug trenches and erected sturdy breastworks, which allowed them to maintain their hold on the ridge. General Lee felt confident that he could overrun the Union force at their weakest point, the center of the ridge. On the morning of July 3, Lee conferred with General Longstreet, who vehemently disagreed with the plan, stating, "General, I have been a soldier all my life. I have been with soldiers engaged in fights by couples, by squads, companies, regiments, divisions, and armies, and should know, as well as anyone, what soldiers can do. It is my opinion that no fifteen thousand men ever arrayed for battle can take that position."

The Bloody Wheatfield changed hands six times over three days of intense combat.

Lee ignored his advice, sending 15,000 of Longstreet and Pickett's divisions across a mile of open ground in a desperate charge aimed at the center of Union forces on Cemetery Ridge, famously known as "Pickett's Charge." Lee had his artillery pound the ridge for two hours before advancing. The Union responded with 100 cannons of their own, firing continuously throughout the morning. However, the Confederate artillery largely overshot the ridge, and the proliferation of smoke and soot prevented both armies from viewing their targets.

Late in the day, as artillery fire from the Federal troops abated and then ceased entirely, Lee convinced himself that the Union batteries had either been destroyed or were low on ammunition. In reality, General Henry Hunt decided to hold his fire in order to lure the rebels closer. As they approached firing range, the Union let loose with a rain of thunder. Cannon balls tore through entire Confederate lines, while the Union's 8th Ohio Infantry Regiment hit them with a surprise musket fusillade from the left flank. Cannister shells that contained deadly shrapnel exploded within their midst, literally tearing their bodies to shreds. After the battle, survivors described collecting unrecognizable body parts that were strewn about the blood-soaked fields. Countless bodies were completely unidentifiable, and the townsfolk buried what remained of them in unmarked graves. In addition, over 5,000 horses had been killed at Gettysburg. It took weeks to clear out the battlefield. It would not be surprising for that level of human suffering and violent trauma to leave its energetic imprint on the hallowed ground.

Civil War photographer Mathew Brady posed for this scene overlooking McPherson's Ridge, just two days after the battle. (*Photograph by Timothy O'Sullivan, 1863*)

An unknown soldier from a New Jersey regiment who had been assigned to bury the fallen soldiers had this to say:

> The dead were everywhere, some with faces bloated and blackened beyond recognition, they lay with glassy eyes staring up at the blazing summer sun; others, with faces downward and clenched fists full of grass and earth, which told of the agony of their final moments. There lay a headless trunk, a severed limb or two, and some lay in grotesque abnormal positions that contorted their human form.

A variety of ghostly figures have been seen in the Valley of Death. Many visitors have spotted the earth-bound spirit of a lone officer sitting astride a white horse. Others have watched entire phantom brigades, silently moving in formation across the fields where they perished. It is common to encounter the energetic remnants of long-dead soldiers in Union and Confederate uniforms marching through the Wheatfield or the Slaughter Pen. In the Valley of Death, invisible figures appear to crawl through the deep grass, leaving behind the imprint of a human body, ghostly apparitions struggling to escape the deadly fire that took their lives.

A lone cannon stands vigil in the Valley of Death.

A statue of General William Crawford stands on the east side of Crawford Avenue. It depicts the officer carrying a bullet-riddled American Flag. General Crawford's unit played a pivotal role in driving the rebel army out of the Valley of Death. The soldier who carries the flag is a lightning rod for enemy fire. When one flag carrier is struck down, another brave man is expected to take up the colors. It was Crawford who seized the flag from a fallen soldier and led his men to victory. In later years, he would become a leading proponent of battlefield preservation. In the many decades after the battle, Crawford's ghost has been seen mounted on a pale white horse, overlooking the field, his head bowed in sorrow. Perhaps the general stands guard over his fallen soldiers, loyal to the end.

Union General Daniel Sickles moved his brigade to the Peach Orchard, exposing both of his flanks to Confederate attack.

Union surgeons conducting an amputation in a hospital tent. (*Photograph by Charles J. Tyson, 1863. Published in Tipton's Photographic Views of the Battle of Gettysburg*)

A monument situated between the Wheatfield and the Peach Orchard is dedicated to the Pennsylvania Light Artillery, known as "Hampton's Battery."

9

The Hummelbaugh Farm

The Hummelbaugh farmhouse, a tiny wooden structure built by German immigrant Jacob Hummelbaugh, was a modest dwelling, even for its time. Located just south of Gettysburg on Pleasanton Avenue, it is now owned and operated by the National Parks Service. It is utilized to house the park rangers who conduct battlefield tours. Any of the rangers who have slept there can tell you that it just does not feel right, with ceilings that are too low, slanted walls that contribute to an overall feeling of claustrophobia, and a dusty attic that nobody cares to explore.

Jacob Hummelbaugh arrived in Gettysburg with his young wife, Sarah, and their little toddler, John. He purchased a large parcel of land, where he constructed a two-story log cabin with a gable rooftop, smokehouse, barn, carriage house, stable, and a chicken coop. After their second child was born, he added another bedroom, a simple lean-to attached to the back wall. Young Sarah passed away in 1853 and Jacob never remarried. His two sons grew up, married, and started their own families, and with the looming Civil War, both men signed up to serve in the Union Army.

When the fighting broke out on the first day of the Battle of Gettysburg, Jacob's farmhouse was situated behind the lines of the Union 2nd Corps. Alone in his home and just sitting down to enjoy lunch, Jacob heard distant cannon fire coming from Seminary Ridge. He soon realized the battle was nearing the edge of town, and when Confederate minie balls repeatedly struck the exterior wall, Jacob wisely decided to abandon his repast. He gathered up some essentials and hurried southward to the home of a close friend, where he stayed for the remainder of the battle. Meanwhile, Confederate soldiers occupied the Hummelbaugh property and converted the farmhouse into a field hospital for the 148th Pennsylvania Regiment. Jacob's living room became an operating theater where army surgeons worked day and night to stabilize wounded men and amputate torn and shattered limbs. The surgeons opened one of the rear windows and carelessly hurled the discarded limbs through the aperture, creating a large stack of grisly remains that piled up against the eastern wall. During the three-day battle, injured rebels were carried to the farmhouse and left outside to await treatment, where they often languished for hours in agonizing pain.

One of the critically wounded was Confederate General William Barksdale, who had led the charge across Seminary Ridge on the second day of battle. He had been struck in a vital organ by a Union minie ball and, bleeding profusely, he was brought to

Confederate General William Barksdale died at the Hummelbaugh farmhouse. His spirit remains at the site, calling out for water throughout the night.

Ohio's monument to Carroll's Brigade stands on East Cemetery Hill. General Barksdale led a failed charge across nearby Seminary Ridge, which cost him his life.

Jacob's home. Survivors at the scene say Barksdale was in a fever-induced state and he constantly cried out for water. No matter how hard his attendants worked to quench his thirst, he only demanded more. The general's wounds were beyond treatment, and he eventually departed this mortal coil. His soldiers buried him in the front yard of the Hummelbaugh farmhouse. On July 4, heavy rains fell, and the Confederate army began their retreat from Gettysburg. Union Cavalry Commander Alfred Pleasanton moved in after the battle and used the farmhouse for his headquarters.

Days later, General Barksdale's wife made the trip to Gettysburg, accompanied by William's favorite hunting dog. She spent the night at the farm, but the loyal hound placed himself at the gravesite and stood sentry throughout the night. In the morning light, the Union soldiers exhumed the body and loaded it onto a wagon bound for Mississippi. The grieving widow then tried to entice the poor dog to leave the gravesite, but the stubborn hound refused to budge. Eventually, she gave up and left with the general's body, believing a kindly neighbor would be sure to look after the dog. The poor hound remained there for days, refusing all food and water. At night, the townsfolk heard his plaintive howls and although many tried to offer him sustenance, he would not take a drop of water. Finally, they found his wasted corpse stretched across the gravesite, and the townsfolk buried Barksdale's dog in the same plot where his master had been interred. But the general's hunting dog remains in Gettysburg to this very day, his earth-bound spirit often heard in the middle of the night, howling in misery for his long-lost master.

Phantom voices, ghostly footsteps, and the plaintive wail of General Barksdale's hound are often experienced in the old barn and farmhouse.

During the battle, a wounded Union soldier had sought shelter beneath Hummelbaugh's windmill. No sooner had he crawled out of sight when it was struck and completely destroyed by an artillery shell. When Jacob Hummelbaugh eventually did return, he found the farmhouse livable but damaged, his chickens gone, and his windmill and barn both destroyed by cannon fire. Although Jacob's two sons had fought for the Union army—one of them seriously injured—he received no compensation for the damage. Jacob died in 1872 and his younger son, John, inherited the farm. The property remained in the family until 1895, when it was sold to the newly created Gettysburg National Military Park. They updated the old building with plumbing, electricity, and modern amenities, and planned to rent it out to the park rangers.

The new tenants soon found they were not alone. Footsteps, cold spots, and phantom voices have been reported over the years by those who have lived at the site, but the most disturbing phenomenon experienced has been the ghostly voice of General Barksdale, calling out in the dead of night for water.

There are countless theories designed to explain why some spirits refuse to move on. Perhaps they never accepted their sudden demise and continue to carry out their life's mission. Some may simply be confused or afraid to meet their maker, others might resent being buried in unmarked graves, never accorded the simple dignity of a grave marker. These unfortunate souls may refuse to rest until their earthly remains are properly interred on consecrated ground.

Army field surgeons in the nineteenth century employed chloroform, ether, and morphine to alleviate pain while performing amputations, but their supplies may have been limited by the circumstances of war. It is quite possible that some Confederate soldiers endured unbearable suffering at the Hummelbaugh farmhouse, which might have infused the entire home with their psychic trauma. Energy can never be destroyed; it just changes form. There is little doubt that many a young soldier spent his last, gasping breath in the Hummelbaugh field hospital.

10

The Death of John Reynolds

In the midst of the bloodiest battle of the Civil War, we find a tender and tragic love story. Major General John F. Reynolds was forty-three and a rising star in the Army of the Potomac. Born to a prominent family in Lancaster, only 55 miles from Gettysburg, he later became a close friend and confidant of General Meade, the commander of the Union Army. Early in 1863, John Reynolds met a young Catholic woman named Catherine Mary Hewitt and they soon fell in love. Within a month, they were engaged to be married, but it was never meant to be. John Reynolds was killed on the first day of battle at Gettysburg, in a courageous stand against overwhelming numbers.

Reynolds and Hewitt had kept their relationship a secret because John was raised Presbyterian, and marriage to a Catholic girl was considered a scandal. In lieu of an engagement diamond, John gave Kate the class ring awarded to him at West Point, and in return she gifted him a crucifix and a heart medallion for John to wear into battle—in essence, a talisman designed to ward off danger. In addition, she had her gold ring inscribed with the words "Dear Kate," and as she watched John worry it onto his smallest finger, she made him a solemn vow; if her beloved was killed in combat, she would dedicate her life to God. Kate vowed to spend the rest of her days in a religious convent, never to marry again.

John Reynolds graduated from West Point in 1841 and spent the next four years in the artillery. He served in the Mexican-American War and established a reputation as a courageous and well-respected soldier. By the time the Civil War began, Reynolds had made brigadier general. He commanded the First Brigade of the Pennsylvania Reserve and saw intense fighting at the Second Battle of Bull Run and again at the Battle of Chancellorsville. He was soon summoned to Washington, where he met privately with President Lincoln. Historians believe that he was offered command of the Union army but turned it down, convinced that previous commanders were too often overruled by Washington politics.

Catherine grew up in Oswego, New York, but was orphaned at an early age, surviving somehow with the aid of an older brother. She was fairly educated, and when she reached her twenties, she traveled to San Francisco with the promise of a position as the full-time governess for a prominent family. The job turned out to be short-lived, and for the next few years, Kate found herself reduced to poverty. She made her way to Sacramento, where she lived on the streets and begged for her meals. There, she met a ten-year-old orphan named Catherine Dunn, and to her credit, she took the homeless child under her wing, essentially becoming her surrogate mother. Kate finally scraped together enough money to

General John Reynolds was killed on the first day of battle. (*Illustrated by Alfred Rudolph Waud, 1863*)

purchase a one-way ticket for the two of them aboard the SS *Golden Age*, bound for New York. It was on that voyage that she met the love of her life. John Reynolds had received orders to leave the West Coast and assume command of the cadets at his alma mater, West Point. John was instantly smitten with the charming young woman, and they soon spent every moment of the six-week voyage together. When Kate arrived in New York, she began a year-long conversion to the Catholic faith, while John served at West Point.

At Gettysburg, Major General Reynolds was in command of the First Core of the Union Army, a force of almost 10,000 men. On the morning of July 1, General Lee's Confederate army forged east out of Chambersburg. In search of food and supplies, they pushed into Cashtown, 8 miles west of Gettysburg. At nearby McPherson's Woods, the 4,000 cavalry troops under Union General John Buford had formed a defensive line, hoping to delay the rebels until General Reynolds arrived with his infantry, now known as "The Iron Brigade." But they found themselves heavily outnumbered and about to cede the high ground along the ridge. General Buford surveyed the battle from atop the copula at the Lutheran Seminary when he spied John Reynolds leading his unit over the lip of the ridge. Reynolds yelled up, "How goes it, John?" Buford replied, "The devils to pay, John."

Reynolds quickly positioned a battery of artillery along the ridge and ordered his infantry to join the fray. The rebel army surged forward once more, forcing Buford's troops to give way but Reynolds, a striking figure mounted atop his white horse, positioned himself near the front lines along McPherson's Ridge, where he inspired the men to fight harder with, "Forward, men. Forward for God's sake and drive those fellows out of these woods!" As he turned to view the rear flank, he was struck in the back of his head by a minie ball fired by a Confederate sniper, thus becoming the first high-ranking officer slain at Gettysburg. He fell from his steed, most likely dead before he struck the ground.

Major General John Reynolds, Army of the Potomac. (*Illustrated by Max Rosenthal, 1897*)

Catherine Hewitt portrait. (*Photograph courtesy of The History Press, Charleston, SC*)

The George George House (oddly, that is not a typo) was positioned in the no-man's land between Cemetery Ridge, held by the Union Army and the Lutheran Seminary, where the Southern troops were advancing. Reynold's men brought the wounded general to George's home, and as he lay dying on one of the beds, his life's blood seeped into the floorboards. This bloody stain has been known to reappear on the aged floor of the George George House at random hours of the night. By morning light, there is no sign of the mysterious mark.

John Reynold's body was initially packed in ice and shipped to his sister's home in Baltimore. It was then embalmed and sent on to Philadelphia, where his younger sisters, Catherine and Ellie, shared a home. Poor Kate learned of John's death in the newspaper and immediately traveled to Philadelphia, appearing at the door of their Spruce Street home, a complete stranger. But they believed her heartbreaking story, having seen the inscription on Kate's ring, still resting on the finger of John's corpse. Kate remained beside her departed lover's body and wept for the entire night. Ellie later wrote to a friend, "John's death was a devastating, crippling loss. We feel for her. 'Tis like crushing the life out of her."

John's body was returned to his hometown of Lancaster and interred on July 4. Kate kept her word and joined the Daughters of Mercy in Emmitsburg, Maryland, where she cared for the sick and the destitute. She served there for four years, eventually transferring to Albany, New York, and teaching at St. Joseph's Catholic School. She later started her own private Catholic school, and over the years, she kept in touch with John's sisters.

When she took her vows at Emmitsburg, Kate was required to give up her worldly possessions, and that included John's West Point ring. It must have tormented her to remove the precious heirloom, but she sent the ring back to Ellie, where it was proudly

The building now used by Servant's Olde Tyme Photos was once a Union field hospital where the body of General Reynolds was briefly stored. His discarnate spirit is said to haunt the building.

displayed on the family mantle. Kate made one request of Ellie: that the family "never let it be tainted by a disloyal hand. He was too true for that." Catherine died of tuberculosis at the young age of forty and is buried in Menands, New York. But it seems her disembodied spirit is not at rest. Her eternal soul has returned to that same building in Gettysburg, the place where her gallant lover spent his last dying breath.

The George George House, a 200-year-old stone building on Steinwehr Avenue, is now the home of Servant's Old Tyme Photos. Television shows and paranormal teams have conducted numerous investigations at the site, and they have captured a number of EVPs (electronic voice phenomena), but most of the ghost stories have been passed along by descendants of the George family. There are three different entities at play. One of the spirits at the Reynolds Death House is fairly aggressive, often playing childish pranks and moving objects around with the clear intention of scaring off investigators. He is known as "The Liar."

Patrons at the photography studio have often seen a tall, bearded man in an officer's uniform believed to be the ghost of General Reynolds. Others have heard horse's hooves, booted footsteps, the whispered voice of a woman in distress, and a few have encountered the apparition of a teenage boy, although he is not wearing a Civil War uniform. His contemporary attire indicates that he may have died more recently, possibly in the 1960s or '70s.

The apparition of a beautiful young woman wearing a nineteenth-century dress is most often seen standing at the window, gazing out at the moonlit street. This forlorn spirit may indeed be the ghost of Catherine Hewitt, a tragic figure so stricken by the loss of her beloved fiancé that she remains by his side, even in death.

General John Buford utilized the cupola atop the Lutheran Theological Seminary (now Schmucker Hall) to survey the battle at Seminary Ridge.

Union soldiers littered the ground at Seminary Ridge, the first major skirmish at Gettysburg. (*Photograph by Mathew Brady, 1863. Published in The Civil War Through the Camera, 1912*)

11

The Jenny Wade House

There are some tragic stories that extend beyond the violent battle for control of Gettysburg in 1863. Virgina "Jenny" Wade was only twenty at the time. She is the only civilian known to have been killed during the fighting, an amazing circumstance on its own. She is buried in nearby Evergreen Cemetery. In 1900, a monument was erected in her memory, and an American flag flies above her gravesite. The only other woman in history awarded that honor was Betsy Ross, the upholsterer credited with designing the earliest version of our Stars and Stripes. Strangely enough, Jenny Wade was also a seamstress.

The Jenny Wade House is now a museum where visitors can view a recreation of her tragic death.

Jenny was born in Gettysburg in 1843, the youngest daughter of James and Mary Wade. James was a tailor but struggled to provide for his family, often disappearing for weeks at a time and running askance of the law. He was convicted of larceny when Jenny was only seven and imprisoned for three years. With no means of support, Mary and her two daughters learned to sew, and they took up the family business. James was eventually released from jail but returned home a changed man. His mental faculties continued to deteriorate until poor Mary was forced to make a difficult decision. She called in the authorities and had him assessed by the courts. Jenny's father was declared mentally unstable and committed to the Adams County Alms House, where he spent the rest of his life.

Jenny's older sister, Georgia, married Louis McLellan, a Union soldier, and they rented a small home on Baltimore Road. On July 1, the first day of the battle, Georgia gave birth to a little boy. Jenny and the rest of her family moved in with Georgia to offer their assistance, as the child's father had gone off to war.

Above left: A family portrait displays Jenny with her two sisters in happier times. Jenny is buried at Evergreen Cemetery. (*Unknown photographer, 1861*)

Above right: The Wade house was struck by minie balls numerous times during the battle. The large hole in the lower right is where the lethal bullet penetrated the door.

Jenny had also fallen in love with a Union soldier, young Johnson "Jack" Skelly. Fate would not prove kind to either of them. On June 15, Jack was wounded by rebel fire at Winchester and captured. They carried him into a temporary field hospital, where the Confederate medic who bandaged his wounds turned out to be Wesley Culp, an old friend of Jack's who had moved to Virginia and later signed up to fight for the South. After the Civil War had ended, Wesley sought out the Wade family and informed them that Jack had died clutching a photograph of his childhood sweetheart Jenny.

On July 1, Lee's Confederate troops stormed into the little town, and the fighting soon spread throughout the entire area. The Federal forces were initially outnumbered, and they retreated to make their stand at Cemetery Hill while awaiting reinforcements. Georgia's home was now at the epicenter of the skirmish. More than 150 bullets struck the northern side of the brick building. Several minie balls pierced the wooden doors, one barely missing Georgia, striking a bedpost while she sat on the bed, holding her two-day-old infant.

Jenny was never one to shy away from duty. She and her mother kneaded dough, then baked and delivered loaves of bread to the Union forces. On the third morning of the battle, a stray bullet drove through two doors and struck Jenny in the back, exploding through her brave, young heart and killing her instantly. Georgia's horrified scream was heard by two Federal soldiers, who rushed into the building and carried her sister's limp body down into the cellar. Nothing could be done for poor Jenny. For a full day, the grieving family held a silent vigil beside her body. In Jenny's apron pocket, they found a photograph of Jack Skelly. The Union soldiers borrowed a casket intended for General Barksdale and buried Jenny in Georgia's backyard. The body was then moved to the German Reformed Church Cemetery. Two years later, the body was interred in Evergreen Cemetery for Jenny's eternal rest.

On the following day, Jenny's grief-stricken mother took it upon herself to finish the task begun by her noble daughter. She baked fifteen loaves of bread from the dough kneaded by Jenny and delivered it to the troops on Cemetery Hill.

Jenny's lifeblood had soaked into the oaken floorboards, where the stain is still visible. The home has since been converted to a museum, where visitors can view a recreation of Jenny's final moments. Staff at the museum are convinced that her phantom spirit now roams the site. They often encounter cold spots, hear footsteps on the cellar stairway, and report objects being moved of their own accord. At times, the faded figure of a young woman wearing a long dress is seen walking across the front yard. Visitors at the site often feel they are being watched.

Paranormal teams and television shows have conducted investigations at the museum and at Jenny's childhood home. One team brought in Karyol Kirkpatrick, a well-known psychic, who declared that there were at least two spirits haunting the museum. She believes one of them is Jenny's father, long denied his beloved daughter's company in life; perhaps he now seeks it in death. A female spirit has also been seen at Jenny's childhood home. It is possible they are one and the same, a restless phantom who clings to the home she knew in life yet is compelled to revisit the scene of her final moments. Or perhaps she waits there for word of her beloved Jack Skelly.

The haunted Jenny Wade house stood empty for a number of years. (*Unknown photographer, 1910. Courtesy of the Marjorie Chase Denoncourt Collection*)

With the exception of Betsy Ross, Jenny is the only civilian woman accorded an American flag at her gravesite.

12

The Louisiana Tigers

Near the base of East Cemetery Hill and just behind the Gettysburg Middle School lies a small, wooded area that residents discuss in hushed whispers. Parents warn their children never to enter the forest, guides who conduct the frequent ghost tours will tell you that it is a paranormal hotspot, a veritable treasure trove of ghostly encounters, glowing orbs, mysterious mists, and spectral apparitions.

It is known as "The Old Grove," and like most of Gettysburg, a pitched battle took place there between a famous Confederate unit from Louisiana and a Union regiment from Ohio. The rebels were greatly outnumbered, and they took heavy casualties. In 1963, during construction of a road through the area, a few dozen bodies were discovered and exhumed. Most of the men were unidentified but believed to be the remains of the most ferocious fighting force ever assembled, the Louisiana Tigers.

The Old Grove has been a favorite area for paranormal teams to conduct investigations. Late at night, you will often see them setting up their various cameras and recording equipment. The most common phenomena captured are brightly colored orbs of light, floating between the trees, but some teams have recorded ghostly voices, musket and cannon fire, and even the sound of a running horse's hooves. Some visitors encounter an amorphous mist that forms about 5 feet off the ground. It is markedly different from the early morning fog that hangs in the wheat fields. The murky haze changes shape, sometimes taking on the vague form of a human body, at other times it curls around the trees as if in search of something, perhaps the long-decayed body of a fallen soldier who lies in an unmarked grave. Although there was an exhaustive effort in late 1863 to find and exhume the bodies belonging to both armies, the National Park Service is not convinced that all the dead were recovered. There still remain a few mass gravesites where decaying corpses were hastily buried in shallow graves, a necessity as the many thousands of bodies had begun to deteriorate, swell, and decompose in the summer heat.

Scattered around the battlefield at Gettysburg are several "Witness Trees," young saplings in 1863 which have endured for more than 160 years. An ancient Elm tree stands proudly at the Grove, one of the few surviving links to the historic event.

Incredibly, the sounds of battle are not the only phenomenon reported at the Old Grove. Many visitors have encountered the ghostly spirit of a young girl reputed to have been driven mad by the unbearable violence. There was only one known civilian casualty in the battle, but it is easy to imagine the horrors of war suddenly thrust upon the normally peaceful village of Gettysburg, and how an experience like that might affect a young teenager. She may have witnessed bodies torn apart by cannon fire, or army surgeons hacking the limbs off of screaming soldiers in a field hospital operating only 30 yards from her childhood home. Driven to the brink of insanity by the horrifying experience, the poor girl might have taken her own life. Perhaps she still roams the bloodied fields and forests of Gettysburg, seeking to escape the madness.

The Middle School has not been spared its paranormal activity. According to one tour guide, teachers and students both tell a strange tale from a wintry morning in 1987. The young history teacher had just handed out a surprise quiz. The teens groaned in unison, picked up their pencils, and buckled down, but there would be no test on this particular day. The teacher turned and walked back towards her desk. Behind her, she heard a collective gasp. She spun around and beheld an astonishing site; the glowing specter of a Confederate soldier had entered the classroom right through the outer wall, glanced at the teacher in apparent confusion, and then ran past the terrified students, disappearing through the opposing wall. Needless to say, the test was postponed, and the kids were sent home with a whopping tale for their disbelieving parents. A phantom soldier traipsing through the classroom certainly tops "the dog ate my homework."

Tour guides will bring their clients to a little-known area behind the Middle School football field, where a small copse of trees stands separated from the forest. Heading east about 150 yards into the woods, the guides then stop in the pitch darkness and point out that 200

Zouave soldiers made up the 114th Pennsylvania Infantry. (*Unknown photographer, 1862. Courtesy of the Library of Congress*)

corpses of the Louisiana Tigers lie in a shallow mass grave beneath their feet. Small wonder that the school and field are haunted. Apparitions of Civil War soldiers have been seen countless times, often in bright daylight. As they excavated the foundation for the school's bleachers in 1963, they discovered fifty-nine more Confederate bodies, placed side-by-side in a shallow trench. They were exhumed and moved to a Southern area cemetery.

The ghostly figure of a disembodied Confederate officer has been known to appear at the Grove, galloping across the field astride his horse, wielding a sword above his head, still trying to direct the furious battle. There was an officer killed while riding a horse on nearby Cemetery Hill. Colonel Isaac Avery was struck by a Union minie ball and thrown from his saddle. Unable to speak, he managed to jot down a simple note and hand it to Major Samuel Tate. It stated: "Major, tell my father I died with my face to the enemy."

Well, what about the horse? Can animals become ghosts? It seems unlikely, but there are theories that may explain the phenomenon. One: the battle at the Old Grove was so violent and horrific that its trauma has infused the very land, in a sense allowing a ghostly echo of the scene to play out repeatedly, for all of time. Two: time is a complete mystery to us. We can measure its flow in minutes or hours, but scientific experiments have demonstrated that it does not flow at a constant speed. It may be possible, under the right conditions, to be awarded a brief window into the past, where the events from those three days in 1863 are playing out. The apparition may not be a ghost at all; just for a single moment, you may be seeing the Confederate officer in action. In the analysis of the paranormal, there are often more questions than answers. All we can do is speculate and observe until modern science finds a way to explain the phenomenon.

A soldier of 10th Rhode Island Infantry Regiment poses in the Zouave uniform. (*Photograph by Frank Rowell, 1862. Courtesy of the Library of Congress*)

Entire books have been dedicated to the Louisiana Tigers, a Confederate unit so infamous that their legend grows with each passing year. With the threat of war becoming a reality in 1861, thousands of young men from Louisiana joined the Army of Northern Virginia, forming quickly assembled units of roughly 100 men, then merging into larger battalions and regiments. They adopted colorful names such as the Atchafalaya Guards, the Carondelet Invincibles, and the Pelican Greys. The Tiger Rifles, assembled by Alexander White, were largely made up of immigrant dockworkers and deckhands, and quite a few felons that had been released from jail. They wore French uniforms in the style of Zouave rather than the standard gray of the Confederate army. Zouave soldiers were recruited from the French Army. They were an elite group of mercenaries bound together by their North African-inspired uniforms, an *esprit de corps*, and a reputation for reckless bravery. General George McClellan once described them as "the ideal soldier."

At Camp Walker, they joined with four other New Orleans companies under the command of Major Roberdeau Wheat, a veteran of the Mexican-American War. The unit of roughly 500 foot soldiers later came to be known as Wheat's Battalion. As they worked their way through Virginia, they developed a sordid reputation for drunkenness, disobeying orders, brawling with other companies, and looting the local towns for alcohol. However, when it came to combat, those aggressive tendencies turned out to be just what the doctor ordered. During the Battle of Bull Run, Major Wheat survived a bullet to the chest, but his Tiger Rifles almost single-handedly repelled the Union force, earning them a new moniker, "The Tiger Battalion."

With Major Wheat out of action, Lieutenant Colonel Charles de Choiseul took command of Wheat's Battalion. As he described the scene, "One night the whole set got royally drunk." Outside the colonel's tent, a drunken foot soldier fired off his loaded musket, barely missing de Choiseul's orderly. He had the man arrested, but that night he found himself challenged by a gang of seven Tigers who demanded the prisoner's release. The colonel knocked one of the men down, but two more threatened to kill him. He drew his musket and warned them to back off. According to de Choiseul, "A big, double-fisted fellow came at me and said, 'God damn you! Shoot me.'" With that, de Choiseul shot him in the face. "He turned as I fired, and I hit him in the cheek, knocking out one upper jaw tooth and two lower ones on the other side, and cutting his tongue. The others retreated, and that quelled the riot." Colonel de Choiseul had earned their respect.

In the Shenandoah Valley, now under General Stonewall Jackson, they joined with the First Maryland Infantry to form the Second Louisiana Brigade and together, they forced a Union retreat. Their reputation became further sullied, as Southern newspapers ripped them for excessive drinking and brawling, stealing livestock, and defying authority.

Only three months later, at the Second Battle of Bull Run, the Louisiana Brigade fought with their typical ferocity but ran out of ammunition. That did not stop them; nothing could rattle these warriors. They gathered rocks and stones and somehow managed to repel the Union force. Collectively, now 12,000 strong, they began to be called the Louisiana Tigers.

They fought in two separate battles at Gettysburg, and as Union army survivors describe the fighting, "We knew the rebels were running low on ammunition. We mowed them down, but they fought even more fiercely, with bayonets, knives, empty muskets, and even swinging dismembered legs at us."

Tigers to the bitter end.

13

Time Slip at Old Dorm

One of the most famous, and certainly among the most horrifying, ghost stories happened at Gettysburg College in 1980. It was here that two administrators got a close-up look at the carnage that took place in 1863.

Originally known as "Pennsylvania College," it was founded in 1832, more than thirty years before the Civil War. The campus consisted of three brick buildings nestled into the center of the town. Pennsylvania Hall, built in 1837, is now home to the administrative offices, but it once served as a dormitory. When the fighting reached the town of Gettysburg in July 1863, the college was packed full of young students, and many found themselves thrust into a living nightmare.

In the haunted cellar of Old Dorm, two administrators stepped into a chaotic scene from the distant past.

At the peak of the fighting, the Confederate army seized control of the dormitory and converted it into a makeshift hospital. Doctors and medics were in short supply. As the wounded and dying soldiers began filling every available room and hallway, the bravest of the students pitched in to help. Union and Confederate soldiers alike were brought in for treatment, often bleeding profusely from lethal wounds, screaming in pain and terror, some already missing injured limbs. There was no time for compassion; their condition was quickly assessed, and the men were sorted into those who could be saved and those with little hope of recovery. Students who had been quietly studying liberal arts only days before now found themselves bandaging wounds in the gory chaos of a military field hospital.

There were no antibiotics, limited anesthetics, and no way to cope with rampant infection. Bandages and bone saws were the tools of choice, and very often, the serrated blade was used on consecutive patients without the time or ability to sanitize the edges. The surgical ward became a blood-soaked nightmare as medics and volunteers carried in the wounded or brought the dead back outside, to be stacked against the side of the building and left to decompose.

This is the very scene that two unfortunate women came upon in 1980. They had been working late into the evening at "Old Dorm" as Pennsylvania Hall had come to be known, filing paperwork and organizing the day's applications in the fourth-floor admissions office. By now, the building was completely empty. They finished their chores, locked the office door, and walked down the hallway together until they reached the elevator. One of them pushed the button for Floor One, they stepped inside the elevator and descended the creaking shaft. But the elevator never slowed as it reached the first floor, sailing past it and coming to a full stop in the darkened basement.

One of the women reached out to tap the button again, but before she could accomplish the task, the doors opened. Instead of a dark and dusty storage room, they found themselves looking into the full light of day, upon a scene of pure horror. Men in Civil War uniforms lay on every available surface, most bleeding profusely and screaming in terror. Students and medics held down thrashing bodies while a doctor performed brutal amputations. More wounded arrived on makeshift stretchers, and volunteers tossed piles of bloodied bandages to the side to make room for the next amputee. The gruesome past had come alive. Frozen in shock, the two women could not move a muscle as they watched the horrifying scene play out. Amid the running, shouting and screaming, they noticed a pile of severed limbs in the corner, oozing blood onto the stone floor.

To their amazement, one of the orderlies happened to look up and then stare at the doorway, his face a mask of bewilderment. He stood up and pointed in their direction. That broke the spell. The younger of the two women punched at the elevator buttons repeatedly until she heard a familiar "ding," and the door finally began to close. The elevator rose to the next floor and opened into their modern-day lobby. They just about tumbled out of it, clutching at each other for support as they shouted for assistance. The college security guard came running over to help, but they could barely get out the words to describe what they had just seen.

Eventually, the two were calm enough to relay their terrifying experience. Later in the evening and now safely at home, they convinced themselves that it had to have been a hallucination. After a few days of prodding, the security officer gradually convinced them to join him and ride the elevator back down to the basement. To their great relief, the doors opened into an ordinary room full of boxes, paper stacks, and filing cabinets. As you might imagine, neither woman visited that basement floor again in the twenty years they continued working at the admissions office.

Like many other buildings in Gettysburg, the college has more than its share of reported phenomena. Students and faculty alike report hearing disembodies voices, footsteps, phantom screaming, and cannon fire. Two other ghost sightings have been reported consistently at Gettysburg College in the years since the historic battle.

On the other side of campus stands Stevens Hall, which boasts of a resident spirit commonly known as the "Blue Boy." His origins date to the latter portion of the nineteenth century, when the building served as a preparatory school that housed only female students. As the tales goes, one January night the campus was struck by a fierce snowstorm. One of the girls was walking through hip-deep snow on her way back to her dormitory when she came across a young boy, suffering in the cold. She scooped up the

The "Blue Boy" peers into the dormitory windows on the upper floors of Stevens Hall.

child, brought him inside, wrapped him in blankets, and warmed up his shivering body. He told the girls he had run away from home. When they informed the house mother of his presence, she promised to investigate the matter and return the child to his home, once the storm abated. The students settled him into an unused room on one of the upper floors, but when the girls returned to check on him, the boy had vanished. The dormitory window had been opened to the howling storm, but they could find no trace of the child.

Years later, two students were awakened by a rapping sound on their window. They sat up in bed and saw a young boy's ghostly features pressed up against the glass, his face a ghastly shade of blue. Other students reported finding the desperate message "Help Me" scrawled into the frost on the outside surface of their window. Objects move on their own, sometimes going missing only to be found weeks later in a different area of the building. The phenomenon is not limited to one room but always occurs on that particular floor.

The Blue Boy makes an occasional appearance at Stevens Hall to this current day.

The first engagement of the battle was fought on Seminary Ridge. The Lutheran Seminary building (now Schmucker Hall) was converted to a field hospital that treated hundreds of wounded soldiers from both armies.

Phantom soldiers sometimes peer out of the Schmucker Hall cupola.

14

The Dobbin House Tavern

By all accounts, the Reverend Alexander Dobbin was a most kind and gentle man. He was also a minister and a well-respected educator, establishing classical schools in both Adams and York counties.

Dobbin was the son of a sailor, born in Londonderry, Ireland, in February 1742. He studied Latin and Greek in Londonderry and then attended Presbyterian Seminary in Glasgow, Scotland. He arrived at the colonies in 1774 with a clear goal, to spread the word of the Gospel and to establish a Classical School, where children studied Hebrew, Latin, and Greek. It would be the first of its kind west of the Susquehanna River. Shortly after his arrival in America, he became pastor of the Rock Creek Presbyterian Church,

That same year, he purchased 300 acres of farmland in what would soon become Gettysburg, and began construction of his farmhouse, which would also house the school. He completed the Dobbin House in 1776—coinciding with the signing of the Declaration of Independence. The rustic tavern still maintains its eighteenth-century charm, featuring stone walls, hand-carved woodwork, seven fireplaces, and antique furnishings.

Reverend Dobbin became a respected community leader. He worked hard to establish an autonomous Adams County in 1800, which had originally been a part of neighboring York County. Dobbin was one of two appointed commissioners who chose Gettysburg to be the new county seat.

Alexander's first wife, Isabella Gamble, bore him ten children. The reverend loved to employ a little word play. When asked how many children he had, he always replied, "Madam, I have nine sons and every one of them has a sister." People naturally assumed that the couple had eighteen children, until he explained with a chuckle that all nine boys had just the one sister. Oddly enough, he ended up with more than eighteen. When Isabella passed away in 1800, he married the widow Mary Agnew, who was struggling to raise nine of her own. Undoubtedly, the reverend had a generous and loving heart.

Small wonder that childish laughter is one of the most common phenomena reported by guests at the Dobbin House Tavern. Late at night, long after the restaurant has closed, doors mysteriously open on their own, and workers often hear young children giggling, followed by the sound of running footsteps.

The Dobbin Tavern may have been one of the earliest stops along the Underground Railroad. On the third floor of the inn, behind a false cupboard, there lies a hidden room where runaway slaves were concealed. The reverend supplied them food and shelter,

The early morning sun lights up the face of the Dobbin House Tavern.

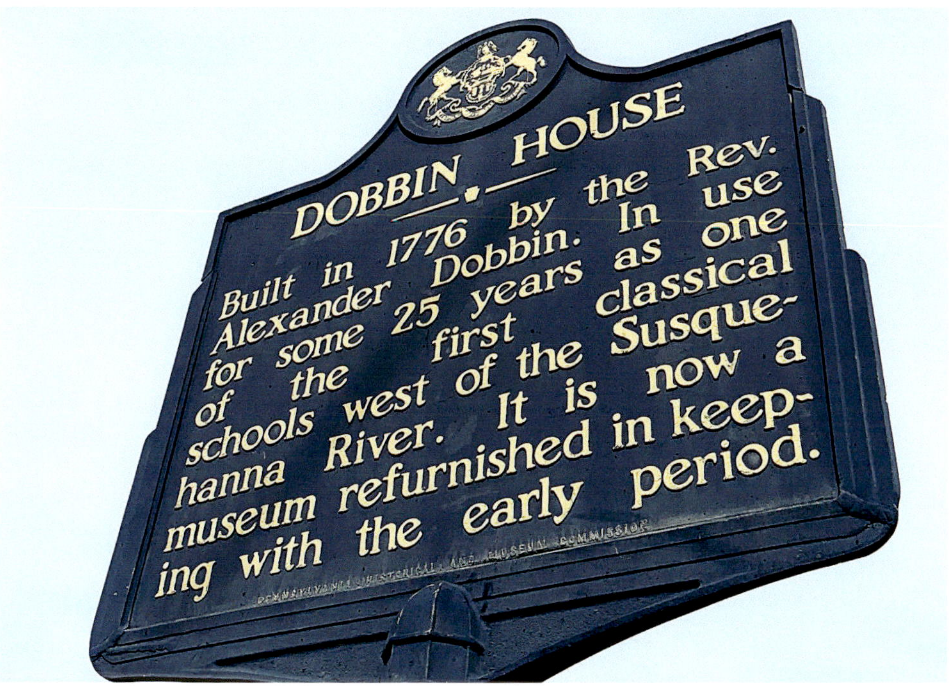

The Reverend Dobbin founded his classical school in 1776.

before they departed for their long and dangerous journey to Canada. At the time, slave hunters could legally recapture them in the Northern states and return them to the South. Situated just north of the Mason–Dixon line, the tavern might have been the first taste of freedom for fugitive slaves. Could that be the reason that the ghostly specters of men and women dressed in tatters and carrying chains often appear at the site? Perhaps some of those lost souls never survived to make their way northward, and in death they returned to the only place where they experienced human kindness.

Like so many other locations during the Battle of Gettysburg, and for weeks afterward, the first floor of the tavern served as a field hospital and operating theater for Union surgeons. Young men suffered unbearable trauma and hundreds died, and many of those tortured spirits have remained on the premises. It is not uncommon for a guest to come across the specter of a Civil War soldier standing in their room.

There are three natural springs flowing beneath the tavern, and that may explain why the site became a hotbed of paranormal activity. Flowing water has often been a source of energy, and some believe that spirits can tap into this continuous supply, which helps them to communicate with the world of the living.

The famous tavern is haunted by at least four different spirits, including the ghost of Reverend Dobbin.

One of the ghostly figures encountered at the tavern is most certainly the spirit of the Reverend Dobbin. Staff and patrons alike describe the apparition as a small, portly man wearing a white wig. He is usually seated in a corner chair, smiling, smoking a pipe, and dressed in breaches with long stockings. Reverend Dobbins died at the age of sixty-seven, while on his way to church. He had contracted tuberculosis, and on that morning, he suffered a severe coughing fit, which may have ruptured a blood vessel. It is my belief that some spirits refuse to move on simply because they are emotionally attached to their location. Reverend Dobbins clearly loved his home and family. It appears that he decided to remain there beyond death to watch over his beloved tavern.

The inn has changed very little since 1863. (*Photograph courtesy of the Dobbin House Tavern*)

15

ROSA CARMICHAEL

The cost of war is always high, and the Civil War was no exception. At Gettysburg alone, there were approximately 51,000 soldiers killed between the two armies—untold numbers who would never see their families again. The repercussions of this brutal war extended far beyond the field of battle. Thousands of families were left fatherless, many with multiple children and most of their widows left with no visible means of support.

The famous story of the unidentified Union soldier killed at Kuhn's Brickyard led to the creation of the National Soldiers' Orphans' Homestead. Clutched in the hand of Sergeant Amos Humiston was the last thing his eyes would ever see, a tintype photograph of his three orphaned children. In the months after the Battle of Gettysburg, the mystery of this soldier's identity had taken on a life of its own, with newspapers across the country displaying the photograph until his young widow in New York, Philinda Humiston, identified Amos and their three children. With the mystery solved, the plight of thousands of other families who were left fatherless became a national crusade.

It was Dr. John F. Bourns who had examined the corpse and discovered the tin photograph, and he now led the charge to assist the children of Sergeant Humiston. According to census bureau data after the Civil War, the number of children living in orphanages had reached an incredible 60,000. Dr. Bourns decided to open an orphanage at the site of battle in Gettysburg, and his first choice to oversee it was the grieving widow Philinda Humiston.

Originally, the two-story home and 2 acres of farmland belonged to J. George Wolf. During the Battle of Gettysburg, the building served as headquarters for Major General Oliver Howard, who commanded the Union Army 11th Corps. It also housed Union sharpshooters who fired on Confederate troops stationed at the southern side of town. Like many other buildings in the little town, it soon became a makeshift field hospital where wounded soldiers were treated, and so many spent their final moments upon this earth. In late 1865, the federal government purchased the property, and in the spring of 1866, Dr. Bourns established the National Soldiers' Orphans' Homestead.

Under Philinda Humistan's guidance, the orphanage functioned as Dr. Bourns had envisioned. The twenty-two children housed at the venue were fed, educated, and clothed, and they appeared well-adjusted to their new situation. Within a few years, occupancy doubled, and a second building was added to the original home.

General Ulysses S. Grant took a strong interest in the nation's orphanages. As part of a national fundraising campaign, he made an appearance at the Gettysburg homestead in 1869. As the demand for shelter increased, the orphanage soon became overcrowded. Eventually, Philinda remarried and moved to Massachusetts.

This is where things turned dark. Dr. Bourns hired a new headmistress by the name of Rosa Carmichael, a woman with a reputation as a strict disciplinarian. For a while, the orphanage operated as expected, but two years later, the residents of Gettysburg noticed that things were amiss.

Philinda had established an annual tradition; the children gathered on the battlefield in July and left flowers for the soldiers who lost their lives in battle. But in July 1867, the children never showed up with their flowers. Concerned neighbors knocked on the orphanage door and were told the children were all being punished. Sometime later, in the dead of winter, those same neighbors heard a child's voice shouting out for help. They found a five-year-old boy locked within the frigid outhouse of the orphanage. He had been there for hours without food and water.

The National Soldiers' Orphans' Homestead was founded in November 1866.

A sixteen-year-old boy who was missing part of one arm managed to escape the orphanage and report to the local police. He told them a harrowing tale; Carmichael had built a dungeon in the cellar of the building where she imprisoned the children who disobeyed. Some were shackled to the wall and left for days, with little food and clothing. Two children very nearly perished but survived by drinking the drainage that seeped into the cellar. Another young girl had been forced to stand atop her desk until she collapsed from exhaustion. Carmichael had hired local teenagers to enforce discipline, a vindictive crew who beat the unruly children with sticks.

Prosecutors brought Rosa Carmichael to trial in 1877, and the sordid details of her cruelty now emerged. Investigators did indeed find a dungeon in the cellar with shackles attached to the fieldstone walls. In her defense, Carmichael's attorney claimed that the chains were already in place and had been used for Confederate prisoners, and that the additional charges were fabricated. Perhaps the testimony of young children was not given the appropriate credence. Incredibly, Rosa was only given a fine, removed from her position, and banished from Gettysburg. There is no historical trace of Rosa Carmichael beyond the trial.

The orphanage closed in 1877 and was sold in 1903, became a bed & breakfast in 1915, and the Soldiers' National Museum in 2013. Museum workers began to tell frightening tales, of phantom voices whispering throughout the night, the sounds of

In 1869, General Ulysses S. Grant visited the orphanage while conducting a national fundraising campaign.

In the haunted cellar, the museum showcases the pit where children were imprisoned. (*Photograph by Jenu Six and Chantal Lynn*)

chains rattling, and children shrieking. Very few employees would enter the dark and foreboding cellar. The building has since closed completely, but the hauntings persist. In recent years, it has become a haven for ghost tours and paranormal investigators.

The most common phenomenon is the sound of childish laughter. Others describe children screaming in pain. Some of the disembodied voices come through very clearly, especially in the basement where the dungeon was located. A white mist often moves through the basement area, sometimes following investigators throughout the cellar. In the darkest corner, where the dirt floor drops into a large pit, investigators encountered a full-bodied apparition—a small child shivering in the corner. The ghostly wraith became aware that he had visitors, and he quickly vanished.

But the most distressing sound of all is the rattling of chains, as though some poor, abused child remains down in the shadows, and is forever condemned to relive his cruel torment. Visitors have taken photographs showing small, indistinct figures that resemble children. A group of paranormal investigators also recorded a woman's voice shouting a vindictive, "Get back!" Those brave enough to descend into the murky depths of

The chains that once shackled the abused children are still on display. (*Photograph by Jenu Six and Chantal Lynn*)

the orphanage cellar often experience a feeling described as "mind-numbing dread." The basement is unusually cold, particularly in the corners. During a Gettysburg ghost tour, one of the guides asked, "Is anybody here?" He received a chilling response, the disembodied voice of a young child replying, "Yes."

Does the discarnate spirit of Rosa Carmichael still haunt the shuttered museum? Local residents and visitors to the Gettysburg area have seen the phantom specter of an old woman wearing a stern expression, peering out of the former orphanage windows. This ghastly sight would be enough to make anyone's blood turn cold.

Was Rosa Carmichael an inhuman sadist, or the victim of a witch hunt perpetrated by resentful children? The answer will never be known, but it may help to explain why her wandering spirit is unable to rest in peace, choosing instead to remain at the abandoned orphanage beyond death, forever haunting the scene of her abhorrent crimes.

16

The Brickhouse Inn

The Brickhouse Inn on Baltimore Street is comprised of two historic buildings, the Victorian House and the Welty House. Constructed as a farmhouse in 1830, the Welty House has changed hands many times, but in July 1863, it was owned by Solomon and Jane Welty, and it housed their five children. The Victorian House across the street was built in 1898 by a wealthy banker, Charlie Toot. He managed the popular tavern, while his family resided in the Welty House. Craig and Marion Schmitz purchased the Victorian House in 1996 and renamed it "The Brickhouse Inn." The two venues now operate as a single unit, a cozy bed and breakfast with antique furnishings. Early innkeeper Charlie Toot is believed to be one of the spirits that remain at the home, although his apparition has been seen in both locations.

The first major battle at Gettysburg took place on July 1. Before the end of the day, Confederate General Henry Heth and his 30,000 troops had managed to overwhelm the Federal force positioned along the western edge of the little town. Heavily outnumbered, the Union troops retreated through the center of Gettysburg. As the Federal force fell back towards Cemetery Hill, the rebels pursued them through the town. Hand-to-hand combat spread throughout the streets and alleyways of Gettysburg, musket and cannon fire struck many of the residents' homes, and families were forced to seek cover where they could find it. The Union troops eventually took a stand at Cemetery Hill, where the high ridge gave them a temporary advantage. The Confederate soldiers now controlled the town, but the battle was far from over. For three days, the rebels occupied several private homes, sometimes employing them as command centers for their officers, and turning others into makeshift field hospitals. Sharpshooters took advantage of the upper stories, where they could aim their sights at Cemetery Hill.

While the Union forces held their ground on the ridge, a small valley at the southern edge of town, beginning at Baltimore Street served as the line of demarcation between the two armies. The Welty House literally became the nexus of the battle, with soldiers firing at one another less than 30 yards apart, Confederate soldiers occupying Solomon Welty's front yard, while Union troops held the back yard. Halfway between the Welty home and Cemetery Hill stood the house where Jenny Wade was felled by a stray bullet. Rebel snipers had occupied the third floor, so it is possible that the fatal bullet was fired from the Welty House garret window. Twenty-year-old Jenny was the only civilian killed during the entire battle.

The ghost of early innkeeper Charlie Toot haunts the Brickhouse Inn. (*Photograph by Glenn Hart, Jr.*)

Solomon Welty quickly gathered up some necessities and ushered his family down into the cellar. John Rupp and his family left their home across the street and took shelter in the Welty basement, where a running spring could supply them precious water for an extended period. Early that morning, John's nearby tannery building had been occupied by the rebels. After the second day of fighting, John saw an opportunity to bring his children to a safer location outside of town. He returned alone and remained in the Welty cellar until the battle ended on July 4. Most of the homes on Baltimore Street had been riddled with bullet holes, struck by cannister shells, or suffered some form of heavy damage. John Rupp's home had been ransacked for supplies, damaged by an exploded cannister shell, and he found the bodies of two Union soldiers lying in his front yard.

At least nine Federal soldiers were killed on the property, and twenty-seven more died nearby and were then buried on the property. Two of the Confederate sharpshooters were struck and killed by Union fire. It is likely that their earth-bound spirits remain in the garret where they spent their final, dying breaths. More than 3,000 Union bodies were later moved to the Soldiers' National Cemetery, but many of the Confederate soldiers are still interred in the Welty House backyard.

Both buildings have their share of paranormal phenomena. Some unusual noises have been described at the Welty House, along with the typical signs of a resident spirit; phantom footsteps, sudden cold spots, and doors slamming all on their own. Guests describe the sound of whizzing bullets flying through the air, others have heard a clicking sound that resembles a flint lighter, often accompanied by the smell of gunpowder.

In the Brickhouse Inn, a local plumber hired to update the bathrooms described reaching for his tools, only to find they had been moved to the far corner of the room. Longtime employee Melanie Driscoll began working at the inn twenty-six years ago, and she now manages the popular venue. She has had quite a few interactions with its mischievous spirits, but she does not find them frightening. She stated, "It all felt light-hearted, like they were getting your attention. Nothing ever felt cruel, or that it had been intended to harm you." She believes there are two different entities at the inn, both older women who may have been long-term employees or tenants.

Late at night, booted footsteps have been heard on the upper floors and in the attic. Some guests report the sound of furniture being moved around on the floor above them. Sometimes, a disembodied voice will call out the name of an employee, and old

Two families sheltered in the Welty House cellar during the Battle of Gettysburg. (*Photograph by Glenn Hart, Jr.*)

innkeeper Charlie Toot's spirit has been known to unlock doors and bark orders at the wait staff, as if he were still running the business.

The Brickhouse Inn's unfortunate location during the furious battle has turned the venue into one of the most haunted sites in all of Gettysburg. Some of these lingering spirits are soldiers, while others appear to be former owners or employees. Perhaps they all have different reasons for remaining. One can only hope that these tortured souls will someday manage to move on to a better place and find some lasting form of peace.

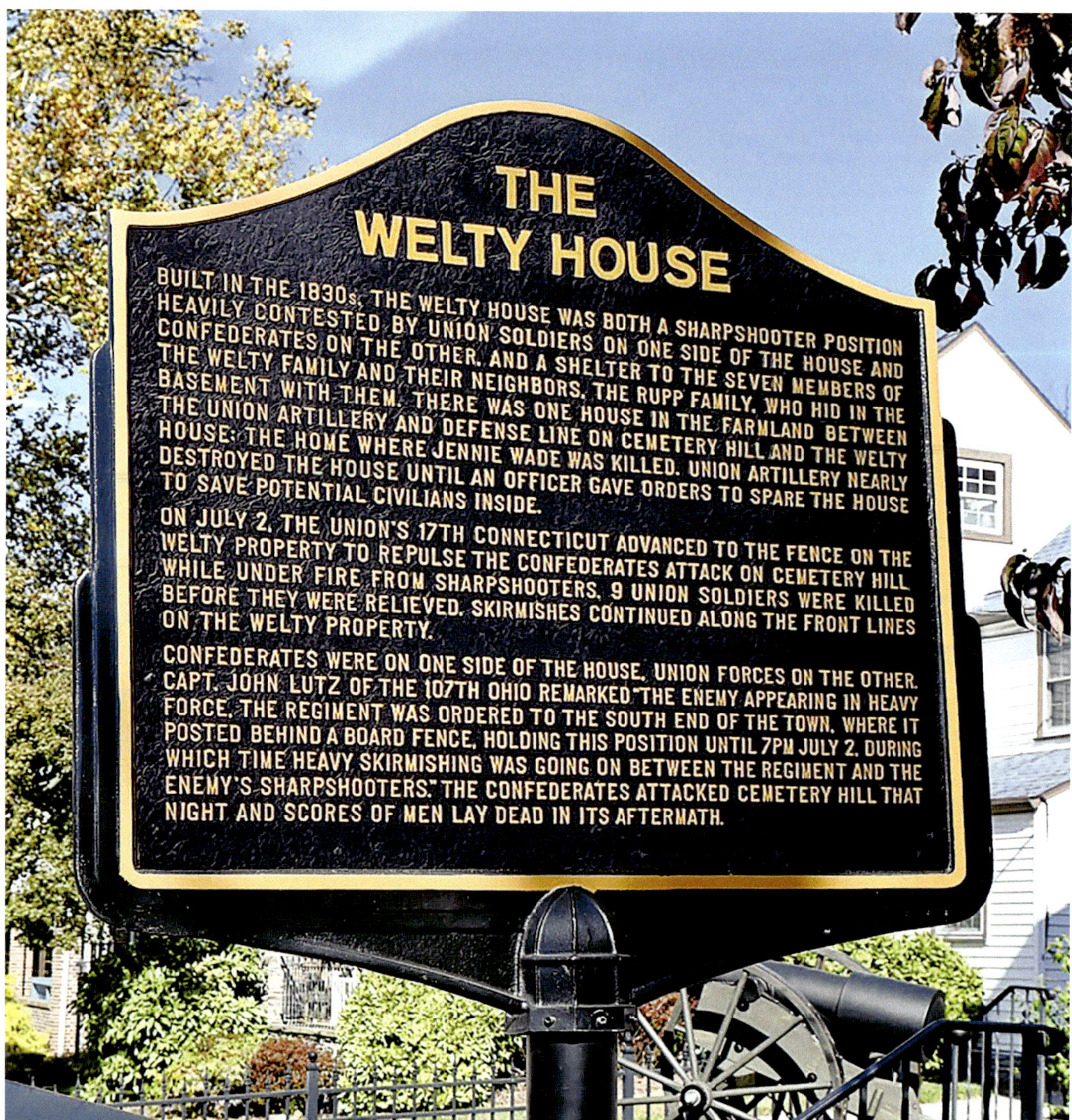

Nine Union soldiers were killed and buried in the back yard of the Welty House. (*Photograph by Glenn Hart, Jr.*)

17

The Weikert Farms

The George Weikert House

At the corners of United States Avenue, Hancock Avenue, and Sedgewick Avenue stands the George Weikert Farmhouse. It is now owned and operated by the National Park Service, and over the years, it has housed many of the park rangers. Each ranger who resided there for a time has a first-hand ghost story, but the most consistent phenomenon described has been a closet door on the second floor that refuses to remain closed.

Time and time again, the residents have closed the stubborn door before heading off to bed. Like clockwork, they found it open when they arose the next morning. Does the farmhouse have a claustrophobic spirit, or just one with a mischievous sense of humor? The answer is unknown and likely to remain so, but the park rangers have given up attempting to keep the door closed. One ranger nailed it shut with a small, wire nail. Once again, in the morning light, he found it wide open.

They often hear booted footsteps pacing across the floor of the attic. Historians found no record of a sniper having been positioned on the top floor during the battle, but it is certainly possible. Perhaps the attic is where some unfortunate soldier met his untimely end.

Ranger Thomas Holbrook has lived at the Weikert House for longer than any other park ranger, almost thirty years. On the northern side of the farmhouse stands a Witness Tree that appeared in a photo taken in 1896. It was likely just a sapling during the Battle of Gettysburg, and the tree is now estimated to be 185 years old.

George and Mary Weikert bought the stone house and 78 acres of farmland from Peter Weikert in 1851. In 1863, George's home was a simple, two-bay granite building. Years later, a second story was added. It lies north of Little Round Top, and when the fighting at Gettysburg intensified at Cemetery Ridge, Union officers occupied the Weikert farm and set up a field hospital. George and his family left for a short time, returning when the three-day battle had ended, only to find their home still occupied by wounded soldiers from both armies. A gruesome stack of discarded limbs lay piled against the side of the farmhouse, oozing blood and decaying in the July heat. Furniture and doors had been destroyed, blood stained the floorboards, and their parlor rug was missing. The rug had been cut into smaller strips and used as a shroud for the burial of Union soldiers, a fact only discovered when the bodies were later exhumed.

On the second floor of the George Weikert farmhouse, a closet door defies all efforts to keep it closed.

The George Weikert farm is displayed in the upper right corner of a 1924 photograph of Little Round Top. (*Photograph courtesy of the National Archives*)

The bothersome spirits may have started haunting the Weikert family right from the beginning, because within a month, George sold the entire property to the New Jersey Brigade, who intended to preserve the hard-fought ground where their unit had lost so many lives. In 1887, it was sold again, this time to the Gettysburg Battlefield Memorial Association.

The Jacob Weikert barn was employed as a field hospital for Union soldiers.

More than 700 wounded soldiers were treated in the farmhouse and barn. (*Photo courtesy of Lynn Light Heller*)

THE JACOB WEIKERT FARM

Jacob Weikert's home on Taneytown Road, just east of Little Round Top, was built in the 1700s as a one-story granite house and enlarged in 1825. The Weikerts bought it in 1840 and began farming the land that surrounded it. Twenty-three years later, their home became one of many makeshift field hospitals for the Union Fifth Core. Over the course of three days, 700 wounded or dying solders were treated in both the house and barn, including four Union officers and Brigadier General Stephen Weed.

The Weikerts had thirteen children and lived on 13 acres of land. They raised farm animals and sold wheat, corn, peaches, and apples. When the Battle of Gettysburg began, they found their homestead in the thick of it, so they packed up their youngest children, a few belongings, and left the farm in the hands of the Federal Army. Jacob and Sarah returned only a day later to a scene of complete chaos. In the words of Sarah Weikert, "We had to pick our steps in order that we might not tread on the prostrate bodies."

Jacob's fifteen-year-old daughter, Becky, and her best friend, Matilda "Tillie" Pierce, witnessed a horrific scene on the evening of July 1. As Tillie described the northern side of the Weikert barn, "Nothing before in my experience had ever paralleled the sight we then and there beheld." She continued, "There were the groaning and crying, the struggling and dying, crowded side by side."

Sarah Weikert and Becky traded shifts and baked bread around the clock for the Union soldiers, but selfless Tillie jumped right into action in the triage, helping to bandage and clean wounds, and even assisting field surgeons while they amputated limbs. She would later publish a memoir about her harrowing experience.

On July 2, wounded men from the First, Second, Third, and Eleventh Corps were now being brought to the Weikert farm. Tillie stated:

The memoir published by Tillie Pierce describes her experience assisting Union surgeons in the Jacob Weikert barn. (*Photo courtesy of Lynn Light Heller*)

> The orchard and space around the buildings were covered with the shattered and dying, and the barn became more and more crowded. The scene had become terrible beyond description. Amputating benches had been placed about the house. I must have become inured to seeing the terrors of battle, else I could hardly have gazed upon the scenes now presented. I was looking out one of the windows facing the front yard. Near the basement door, and directly underneath the window I was at, stood one of these benches. I saw them lifting the poor men upon it, then the surgeons sawing and cutting off arms and legs, then again probing and picking bullets from the flesh.

The bodies of Lieutenant Charles Hazlett and Colonel Patrick O'Rourke—both killed in battle—were laid upon the Weikert front porch. General Weed was alive when carried into the farmhouse, but he eventually succumbed to his injuries. All in all, 100 Union fighters were buried in the Weikert's fields. Most were later exhumed and transferred to the Soldiers' National Cemetery.

In the days and weeks after the carnage had ended, the Weikert family began hearing voices in the dark of night, men screaming in pain, or calling out for help. Footsteps continually echoed throughout the farmhouse and barn. Spectral figures dressed in Union army blue would appear in the old barn, and in many other areas of the farm.

Tillie Pierce's memoir has been an invaluable tool for historians, a first-hand account of the true horrors of war, the nightmarish conditions so vividly described as seen through the eyes of a fifteen-year-old girl. It is not surprising to find the energetic trauma of these events imprinted into the very fabric of the Weikerts' farmhouse and barn, to be replayed for generations to come, and quite possibly, for eternity.

Spectral apparitions still appear at the Jacob Weikert farmhouse. (*Photo courtesy of Lynn Light Heller*)

18

SPANGLER'S SPRING

The skirmishes at Spangler's Meadow, Culp's Hill, and Spangler's Spring took place early in the three-day engagement for control of Gettysburg but all three would prove crucial to the much larger battle that occurred on July 2, which would involve the bulk of both armies.

Historians still debate the sequence of events surrounding Culp's Hill. On the first day of fighting, the Confederate army had far greater numbers massed along the western edge of Gettysburg, while the Army of the Potomac would not arrive in force until late in the day. The Union troops, commanded by General Winfield S. Hancock, had made their stand on the high ground at Cemetery Hill, barely holding the strategic ridge by constructing fortified breastworks that frustrated the advance of the rebels.

Major General Richard S. Ewell, in command of the Confederate Second Corps, had been ordered by General Lee to assault and take Culp's Hill and Cemetery Hill, if it could be done without major losses, but to avoid at all costs a "general engagement" until Lee had his full complement in position for the second day of battle. General A. P. Hills' troops had arrived from the west and were ready to add support, if necessary. Confederate General Edward Johnson had surged into Gettysburg, driving the Union forces out of the small town, just as the sun was beginning to set.

If the rebels had been able to take Cemetery Hill on the first day of fighting, the Battle of Gettysburg may well have turned out differently. General Ewell sent scouts to the top of Culp's Hill, and they found the battlements unguarded. Ewell was preparing an assault upon the hill when he received word that a large body of Union soldiers was approaching from his rear, forcing him to defend on two fronts. He called off the attack.

Early that same morning, Lieutenant Colonel Charles Mudge, commanding the 2nd Massachusetts Infantry had been ordered to cross Spangler's Meadow and attack the Southern forces on the side of Culp's Hill, a virtual suicide mission, as the rebels were entrenched on higher ground and well protected by a large field of boulders scattered along the hillside. The 27th Indiana joined with Mudge's unit, but the two regiments amounted to 600 men against 1,000 Confederates made of Smith and Steuart's Brigades. Still, they obeyed their orders and attacked the hill, repeatedly being driven back to Spangler's Meadow. The Confederates, emboldened by their success, advanced across the meadow but a long stone wall now protected the Union soldiers. They fought for hours across the blood-soaked meadow, neither side able to gain any footing. As night fell, both sides retreated to their original positions. Spangler's Spring stood between the two forces. Colonel Charles Mudge had been killed, and the lone Union brigade still held both Cemetery and Culp's Hill.

Water still flows through Spangler's Spring, but the town of Gettysburg erected a stone archway around it in 1895, and they covered the spring with a metal grate. Three bronze plaques placed around the arch memorialize the soldiers who fought and died at the site. Visitors can descend three steps and view the underground spring, but the National Park Service now prevents access, fearing contamination of the ground water.

There are two prominent legends associated with Spangler's Spring. Water, of course, is the most valuable commodity to a fighting army. There is little doubt that both Union and Confederate soldiers accessed the site to fill their canteens. They traded ground and positions several times over those three long days of brutal warfare.

The first legend is a bit of a stretch. After two days of intense battle, both sides were spent and exhausted. With the Union controlling Culp's Hill and the Confederates hunkered down behind Spangler's Field, it would have been a dangerous endeavor for any soldier to cross the field and obtain water. So, one side raised a white flag and suggested a parley. They met at the spring and agreed to a single-night truce, allowing

The "Lady in White" haunts the battle-worn hills and fields surrounding Spangler's Spring.

both units to fill their canteens without the risk of being killed. As they gathered around the spring, the soldiers socialized and traded stories. Once the dawn arrived, the fragile truce ended. As I stated, not a lot of historians give the tale any credence. A soldier conversing with the enemy would more likely have been shot for his trouble.

A more enduring legend involves the "Lady in White," a ghostly figure who shows up as a flowing white mist near the spring. The fog slowly forms into a human torso and, finally, the glowing figure of a young woman wearing a white dress. She carefully searches the hard-fought terrain, occasionally bending to inspect something more closely and then she slowly vanishes. Sightings of the figure have been reported many times over the years, in both day and night, although the park, which was once open until 10:00 p.m., is now closed to visitors after the sun has set. Some witnesses also describe a feeling of intense sadness that envelopes the entire field.

A second interpretation paints the specter as a jilted woman who died long before the Battle of Gettysburg. For months, she and her secret lover had been enjoying a sordid affair, meeting weekly at the spring when the clock turned to midnight. But her lover arrived one night to tell her that their tryst had been discovered, and he could no longer continue. Heartbroken by this betrayal, she returned the next night and committed

On July 1, Union and Confederate forces battled to a stand-off at Spangler's Meadow.

suicide by the side of the spring. Her grieving spirit is said to return whenever a promise has been broken, and she then kneels above Spangler's Spring, crying in bitter anguish.

Writer and historian Mark Nesbitt was approached at one of his lectures by a couple who informed him that the Lady in White had been seen quite often within their home, located only a few hundred yards from Spangler's Spring. Mark organized an investigation, inviting a local medium to join them. When asked if she felt that a female spirit dressed in white had once lived on the second floor, the medium answered, "Yes, she is a nun."

Many of the Sisters of Charity housed in Saint Joseph's Convent in Emmetsburg rushed to the Gettysburg battle site to offer their assistance and pray for the souls of the young warriors. There were no women involved in the battle, but once the fighting had ended on July 3, it was left to the townsfolk to clear out the remaining bodies. Much of the area had once been fertile farmland, and farmers needed to resume planting crops in order to survive the coming winter. They spent weeks at the ghastly chore, collecting body parts and digging graves, mostly for the Confederate soldiers. As the corpses began to decompose, the smell of rotting flesh in the summer heat must have been unbearable. Gettysburg townsfolk wore rags or handkerchiefs across their mouths containing peppermint or crushed wildflowers. It was the only way to endure the awful stench.

The Union army remained for a week to respectfully bury their own soldiers. It is very possible for a local woman to have been searching desperately for her missing friend, brother, or lover. Her psychic pain may have infused the hallowed ground with a permanent record of her suffering, causing it to play out in an endless loop. Perhaps the Lady in White is unwilling to leave this earthly plane until she learns the tragic fate of her young soldier.

At the base of Culp's Hill stands a monument to Union General Henry Slocum.

19

The Farnsworth House Inn

The Gothic-style brick Farnsworth House Inn situated on Baltimore Street is now a popular bed and breakfast, but it is more widely known as the most haunted hotel in Pennsylvania. The current owners, Loring Schultz and his extended family, profess that no less than sixteen spirits reside on the premises, each with their own unique personality. Full apparitions of both Union and Confederate soldiers have been encountered over the years, as one might expect for a building that once served as a field hospital for both armies. Farnsworth House staff and patrons experience some form of paranormal phenomena on an almost weekly basis. Cynthia Codori-Schultz offers guided ghost tours of the quaint historic inn and the nearby battlefield.

Many consider the Farnsworth House Inn to be the most haunted venue in Pennsylvania.

The Farnsworth House has boasted four owners since 1800. The original plot of land was purchased by the Reverend Alexander Dobbin, one of the earliest pioneers to settle in Gettysburg. In 1810, Dobbin sold the lot to John F. McFarland, who constructed a two-story home, then added a second building, a sturdy brick structure, in 1830. John passed away in 1851 and the mortgage was taken over by the Bank of Gettysburg. For a time, the building served as a tannery, a restaurant, a lodging house, a tavern, and a slaughterhouse. Harvey Sweney assumed the mortgage in 1852, and the historic venue became the Sleepy Hollow Lodge.

In 1909, Sweney sold the inn to George and Verna Black, and the couple ran it for forty years. When Verna died, it was passed down to their daughter, Sara Gideon Black. Sara is believed to be one of the many spirits who remain at the inn. In 1972, the old building was scheduled for demolition, but Loring Schultz purchased and then restored the inn to its 1863 appearance. Shortly after moving in, Loring realized why the building had changed hands so often. His charming venue contained a host of other-worldly entities. But over the years, the family has learned to live with them. At ninety-two, Loring still comes in daily to assist the family with general maintenance.

The specter of a nineteenth-century woman often appears within the Sara Black Room.

During the Civil War years, the inn was run by Harvey Sweney and his family. After the battle, the Sweneys found their home riddled with bullet holes, many still visible to this day. A cannonball had torn a large hole in the roof, landing in the attic. Over the years, the owners have collected roughly 135 bullets from various areas around the property. Early in the three-day battle for control of Gettysburg, the Union army had established command of the high ground at Cemetery Hill. The Confederate army, 30,000 strong, had swept into Gettysburg from the northwest and invaded many private homes, searching for food and supplies. They commandeered Sweney's building and turned it into the headquarters for Brigadier General Lewis Armistead. The inn was an ideal location to position snipers in the garret window of the attic, where they could pick off Union soldiers at Cemetery Hill, only 500 yards away.

Unfortunately, one of the stray shots passed through the front door of a residential home, killing twenty-year-old Virginia "Jenny" Wade where she stood in her sister's kitchen, baking bread for the Union army. Young Jenny was the only civilian casualty of the three-day engagement. For two days, the Union and Confederate forces surged and retreated over a 5-mile square battlefield, the fighting so savage and brutal that one blood-soaked field later came to be known as "the Slaughter Pen."

Civilian Jenny Wade may have been killed by a sniper's bullet fired from the garret window.

On July 3, after pummeling the Union position at Cemetery Hill with heavy artillery, Commander Robert E. Lee ordered General Longstreet to join with General Pickett's two brigades and penetrate the center of the Union troops holding the ridge. Longstreet felt that the plan was suicide, and he openly challenged Lee but could not persuade the stubborn commander to reconsider. His famous quote, addressed to Lee, stated: "It is my opinion that no fifteen thousand men ever arranged for battle can take that position."

They formed a mile-long line and marched the rebel troops across an open field, which proved to be disastrous. Delayed by broken fences and hilly terrain and blinded by the smoke from the constant shelling, they took heavy fire from two directions and were finally forced to retreat, having already lost 60 percent of their number. This skirmish, famously known as "Pickett's Charge," is considered a major turning point in the battle and, consequently, the entire Civil War. General Lee was eventually forced to withdraw and reconsider his attempt to reach Washington, D.C., via Pennsylvania. During the charge, Confederate Brigadier General Lewis Armistead had been mortally wounded. Armistead was carried back to the Sleepy Hollow Lodge, where he soon died.

Union army Captain Elon Farnsworth had been promoted to brigadier general a mere four days ago. Only twenty-five at the time, his promising military career would prove fleeting. As the Confederate forces retreated towards Emmitsburg Road, he was ordered to engage their right flank with a handful of men, all that remained from the

The spirit of a Union soldier occasionally appears within the haunted mirror. The proprietors have named him Walter. (*Photograph courtesy of the Farnsworth House Inn*)

1st Vermont Regiment. The numbers and terrain favored the rebels. They sheltered behind trees, rocks, and fences and picked off the Union's charging cavalry, including Farnsworth, who was struck five times and thrown from his steed. Nearly all of his men perished. Elon Farnsworth was the son-in-law of the inn's first owner, John McFarland. In tribute to the young General's valor, the Farnsworth House Inn now bears his name.

While the battle raged and young men died by the thousands, the Sweney's basement was used to store the Confederate bodies before burial. At one point, it was estimated that twenty-one cadavers lay heaped against the eastern wall of the fieldstone cellar. On the third day of fighting, the Union forces stormed the building and killed or dispelled the rebel sharpshooters. Late that night, in heavy rains, General Lee gathered his forces and began their long retreat, under the cover of darkness. Union soldiers took over the building and once again, the lower floor was converted to a makeshift field hospital. Army surgeons were often assisted by local residents as they bandaged soldiers' injuries, or hacked off wounded arms and legs, often with the same bloodied saw. Ordinary townsfolk with little or no medical training found themselves first-hand witnesses to the terrible cost of war.

Unable to identify the many spirits that frequent the inn, the current owners have assigned them names. Walter is the bearded Union soldier most often seen in the basement. Sissie is the matronly woman usually found in the kitchen, and Jeremy is a small child, considered to be the most active ghost at the inn.

The cellar features a Victorian-era funeral scene, complete with a shrouded corpse.

Several visitors at Gettysburg have taken exterior photographs of the Farnsworth House Inn, only to discover that their candid photographs revealed a strange anomaly, the pale, scowling face of an eighteenth-century woman peering out of a second-story window. This is the Sara Black Room, the most active location at the inn. Late at night, frightened guests in the Black Room have experienced disembodied voices, soft footsteps, and the pungent scent of perfume. Many visitors claim they are being watched, sometimes objects move around or go missing, or they feel a general heaviness within the room. One corner in particular seems to exhibit very unusual phenomena. It is often many degrees colder than the rest of the room and occasionally, the haunting specter of an old woman is seen standing in the shadows, glaring at the room's startled occupants.

The dining room and kitchen are said to be haunted by a matronly figure who has been known to push cooks and waitresses out of her way, as if impatient to get on with her tasks. She is often observed leaning over the shelves, deep in thought and possibly planning her next meal. Workers have encountered her in the hallways, dressed in nineteenth-century clothing and appearing as solid and substantial as the hotel guests. Perhaps she served as headmistress of the inn during her day. And now, she remains at the old tavern indefinitely, making sure the meal preparations are to her liking. She has been known to pull on apron strings, sometimes hard enough to spin a staff worker around. Imagine their consternation, as they turn to express their anger and find there is not a soul in sight. But the crew has gotten used to their spirits. They really do not have much of a choice.

For those brave enough to sleep in the Sara Black Room, which is situated beneath the attic once occupied by Confederate snipers, they may find themselves serenaded at 4:00

A ghostly hand reaches out to touch the arm of an unwary visitor reflected in the haunted mirror. (*Photograph courtesy of the Farnsworth House Inn*)

a.m. by the eerie sound of a jaw harp. Perhaps the specter of some lonely rebel sentry stands guard just 12 feet above their heads, passing the time by playing the somber tunes that he enjoyed in life. Three rebel soldiers were killed in the attic as they fired upon the Union troops at Cemetery Hill. Very often, patrons in the Black Room hear their cadavers being slowly dragged across the floor. In the Eisenhower Room, you are likely to experience the strong scent of cigar smoke. A grizzled officer in the gray uniform of the Confederate army will often make an appearance, usually in the dead of night.

Loud, banging noises are frequently heard in the corner room on the second floor. Its spectral visitor is an eight-year-old boy known to have been killed at the site. He has been seen in other areas but seems to favor that one room, so the Schultz family named it after him. In the Jeremy Room, patrons describe the chilling sound of childhood laughter, and thumping footsteps running down the hallways at ungodly hours of the night. Coins left on the dresser are moved around and occasionally found neatly stacked in the center of the room. Some visitors bring toys and leave them out for Jeremy. In the morning, they are found spread across the floor.

Jeremy died in 1866. He had been hanging out with a group of older boys, who enjoyed playing a dangerous game of "horse tag." The young teens would wait for a horse-drawn carriage to come by, then run into the street and slap the lead horse on its hind quarters, causing it to bolt forward or suddenly rear up. When it became Jeremy's turn, he ran out and struck the horse but lost his own footing in the muddy street, tumbling underneath the carriage, where he was trampled. The townsfolk carried Jeremy into the foyer of the inn and called for a doctor, but the poor child bled out

Minie balls struck the exterior wall repeatedly during the battle, leaving pockmarks that are visible to this day.

before he could be helped. He remains at the building where he tragically expired, playing mischievous pranks on the unsuspecting patrons of the inn. Jeremy's mother had passed away at a young age, and tour guides have noted that he often is drawn to young girls with blonde hair. He enjoys pulling on their locks or gently stroking their honey-sweet hair.

In the McFarland Room, the spirit of a woman wearing a long white dress sometimes makes an appearance. Sleeping patrons have reported being awakened at midnight by the sudden movement of their beds, as if some phantom figure had just sat themselves down on the end of the mattress. The mysterious woman is younger than the matronly cook and a lot more friendly, but the phantom specter does not seem to be aware that she has passed beyond this mortal coil.

The basement is the most active area, by far. On the first day of battle, the Confederate troops had managed to drive the Union lines all the way back to Cemetery Hill, where they took a stand on the high ground. The townsfolk found themselves in the middle of the fray, and those who had been roaming the streets scrambled for shelter. Harvey Sweney opened his doors to rescue twelve neighbors. When the Confederates soldiers

Mediums have encountered aggressive spirits in the Farnsworth House cellar.

took control of the building, they forced the tenants down into the cellar, illuminated only by candlelight. The rebels carried their wounded men into the front parlor and stabilized them to the best of their abilities. As the injured soldiers lay dying, their lifeblood seeped in-between the floorboards and dripped down into the basement, forcing Harvey and his guests to endure a literal rain of blood. The wounded rebels that died were carried down to the cellar and piled up in a small storage room.

This gloomy chamber was open to the public until 2005, when two different tour groups emerged from the room with scratch marks on their bodies. Cynthia called in famous psychic and paranormal investigator Lorraine Warren. Lorraine validated the presence of harmless spirits within the Farnsworth House, but in that basement room she felt something profoundly threatening, and she heard the guttural sound of a growling animal. Since that night, the storage room has been locked and barricaded.

You can tour the Farnsworth House Inn without having to spend your night in a haunted room. The cellar display alone is worth the price of admission. The Gothic Victorian decor includes a wall of framed period photography, a stuffed vulture, a stone gargoyle, and a nineteenth-century funeral scene containing a black wooden casket complete with a ghastly corpse.

To the side of the coffin is a large mirror with an ornate frame and a sordid history. It once housed the portrait of young Clarence Collins, a troubled man who lived an extremely violent life and committed murder in 1918. His pious Puritan parents disowned the man, tearing out his portrait and then bringing the frame to a local merchant, who converted it to a mirror. As soon as they brought the mirror back into their home, they were tormented by knocking sounds, disembodied voices, and dark, spectral figures. They sold the cursed object to an antique dealer, who held it in storage for seventy years. Cynthia Codori-Schultz came across the artifact and purchased it for display in the inn's haunted basement. It has not let her down. Frequently, photographs taken at the mirror display ghostly faces, or the apparitions of soldiers in Civil War uniforms.

Numerous paranormal investigators have tried their hand at identifying the Farnsworth House spirits. April Busset, known as "The Psychic Housewife of New Jersey," heard the message, "Help me" through her Spirit Box. When she asked, "How can we help you?" she received a clear reply, "The sickness!" Psychic medium William Stellman caught the image of a spectral woman in the haunted mirror, and Ami Bruni of the paranormal series *Kindred Spirits* theorized that the mirror serves as a portal to the spirit world.

I spent a single night at the Farnsworth House, sleeping in the Sara Black Room. Although I recorded audio and filmed for seven hours with infrared cameras, I captured very little evidence. Ghosts appear on their own schedule, not ours. In the morning, I enjoyed a delicious breakfast served in the Sweney Tavern, tastefully decorated with Civil War memorabilia. The Farnsworth House Inn is a veritable treasure. Filled with Victorian-era antiques, ornately framed paintings, and vintage photographs, the venue will transport you to the nineteenth century. And you may also encounter a spectral entity that hails from the distant past.

20

The Daniel Lady Farm

The Daniel Lady Farm, now owned by the Gettysburg Battlefield Preservation Association, was occupied on June 26, 1863, by Confederate General Edward Johnson and converted to his personal headquarters. Robert E. Lee had his advance scouts assessing the area east of Gettysburg for days before the impending battle. Lee had determined that it was crucial for the South to control nearby Culp's Hill before they fully engaged with the Army of the Potomac. If the Confederates could take Culp's Hill, it would disrupt the supply line for the Union Army, preventing them from acquiring ammunition, artillery, and medical supplies. On July 1, only a small contingent of Federal soldiers occupied the hill.

A field hospital inside the Daniel Lady barn served to treat the enlisted men.

The Lady family was about to celebrate their fourth child's birthday, when a Confederate officer appeared at their door with 5,000 troops in tow and informed the family that they would have to vacate their home. General Robert E. Lee then arrived and held a conference in the family's parlor with General Edward Johnson and General Richard Ewell in order to plan their strategy. Daniel and Rebecca Lady took their seven children to a neighbor's home and awaited the outcome of the battle.

On the following day, thousands of troops made up of General James Walker's "Stonewall Brigade," Nicholl's Louisiana Brigade, Colonel Snowden's Artillery Battalion, and "Maryland" Steuart's Brigade, formed up east of the farm and began their assault on Culp's Hill, a battle that Lee assumed would be an easy victory for the Confederate Army. He was badly mistaken.

After hours of heavy fighting, the Confederates were forced to retreat to the Lady farm, where they set up a field hospital in the farmhouse for treating officers, and a second one in the barn for the enlisted men. Hundreds of wounded soldiers passed through those doors, some on the verge of death, others screaming in pain as their life's blood seeped into the floorboards. Historians contend that the two field hospitals treated more patients than any of the others at Gettysburg.

Soldiers tore apart furniture to be used as firewood and removed doorways to employ as stretchers and surgical tables. They covered the floor in hay to prevent their doctors from slipping on the blood that constantly dripped from open wounds. Surgeons opened the first-floor windows to prevent the build-up of fumes from the chloroform employed as anesthesia, while conducting hasty amputations. The soldiers' discarded limbs were hurled out of the open windows, and they formed a large pile in the yard. These appendages were later buried somewhere on the property. The men who succumbed to

Daniel Lady helped the Union soldiers bury twenty-two Confederate bodies on his property.

their injuries were wrapped in blankets and placed on the front porch. While all this was happening, the battle raged on, and an occasional artillery shell struck the house and barn. In later years, two different cannister shells were still embedded in the side of the building.

After three days of intense battle, General Lee was forced to abandon his invasion of the North and begin his retreat. When the Lady family was able to return home, they found their farmhouse in ruins, much of their furniture destroyed, bloodstains covering the floors, their livestock consumed or stolen, and according to one source, a dead body was left in a second-floor bedroom. After the battle, Daniel Lady assisted the rebels to bury thirty-seven of their dead on his property. Twenty-two were never identified, and a number of those bodies remain there to this day. In later years, most of the Union bodies and some of the Confederates were exhumed and transferred to other cemeteries.

After the battle, the northern portion of the field (owned by farmer George Wolff) became the site of the Camp Letterman Field Hospital, the largest facility of its kind, which treated almost 4,200 patients. It was the only location where soldiers from both armies were treated for their wounds, chosen because of its proximity to the railroad, which allowed them to bring in supplies and transport survivors to their homes.

Confederate surgeons treated officers inside the farmhouse. Amputated limbs were hurled through an open window.

However, descendants of the Lady family can tell you that some of those departed souls refused to leave. Over the years, they have encountered the ghosts of both Union and Confederate soldiers in the barn, the farmhouse, and in the fields where they were laid to rest. Are these fallen warriors longing to have their bodies identified, are they searching for their missing limbs, or are they unable to come to grips with their sudden and violent deaths, so young in life and so far from their homes? We will never know the answers.

One of the spirits is a Union officer, a bearded specter commonly believed to be General Richard S. Ewell, a man perhaps haunted by his own failure to take Culp's Hill and tormented by the high cost of his failed campaign, a toll paid in life and limb.

The two field hospitals at the farm treated more soldiers than any of the others at Gettysburg.

The Daniel Lady farm now serves as a museum, recreating the operating theater during the Battle of Gettysburg.

The ghostly figures of long-dead, rebel soldiers roam the fields by night. A small plaque marks the site where they fell in battle.

21

The Mansion House

There are only five colonial taverns in all of America that have been running continuously since the 1700s. Southwest of Gettysburg stands one of them, the stately Mansion House in Fairfield. For many years, this historic Adams County venue was known as the Fairfield Inn. The current owners, George and Cynthia Keeney, purchased the old tavern in May 2020 and decided to restore the original name. Constructed in 1757 on a 123-acre dairy farm operated by the Hoffman family, it came to be called "the Mansion House" because it was the largest structure in Fairfield. The stone building features a gable rooftop and a unique, three-story Victorian Gothic-style porch.

The ghostly specter of a young woman who took her own life at the Mansion House still wanders the third-floor hallways.

In 1786, Squire William Miller filed for the Mansion House to operate as a tavern, the first in the Gettysburg area. Once the license was granted, the Mansion House also became a stagecoach stop. Miller had served as a captain in the Colonial Army and he was a staunch Federalist. He later became Pennsylvania's first state senator.

Charles Mason and Jeremiah Dixon completed their survey in 1765, which defined the Mason–Dixon Line. Originally the boundary between Maryland and Pennsylvania, it later became the dividing line between the slave-owning states below it and the free-soil states above it. While working in the area, Mason and Dixon stayed at the Mansion House. At the completion of this project, the Mansion House became part of Pennsylvania.

During the Civil War years, the Fairfield Inn was owned by Peter Shively. Situated just north of the Mason–Dixon line, it became an early "station" on the Underground Railroad, sheltering runaway slaves on their danger-filled journey to freedom. Like so many other large buildings in Gettysburg during and after the famous battle, it served as a temporary field hospital for wounded Confederate soldiers.

On the third day of the Battle of Gettysburg, a brief but brutal cavalry skirmish took place 2 miles from the property, killing or wounding forty-seven Confederate soldiers. Most of the injured were carried to the Fairfield Inn and treated by field surgeons. Many young soldiers lost an arm or a leg, their limbs amputated with minimal anesthesia, and the army surgeons had no antibiotics to combat infection. Rebel soldiers that were killed in battle were often buried in temporary graves. Some, but not all were later reinterred in Southern state cemeteries.

On July 4, General Lee began his retreat to Virginia, stopping for a meal at the Fairfield Inn and then parading the remaining soldiers of the Army of Northern Virginia past the venue. Many of the wounded rebels remained at the inn until they were well enough to travel. Others succumbed to their injuries and were later buried at the site.

A skirmish involving Stuart's Cavalry resulted in forty-seven wounded soldiers. Eleven of them died at the Mansion House.

For many years after the war—and to the current day—the inn has experienced rampant paranormal activity. Guests and employees describe bedroom doors opening of their own accord, disembodied voices, cold spots, and glowing orbs floating through the hallways and kitchen area. The proprietors believe that many of their spectral visitors are the disembodied souls of young Confederate soldiers. Hastily buried and long forgotten, their bones interred so far from their homes and families, it is no surprise that their spirits cannot rest in peace.

The old inn may have been haunted long before the Civil War broke out. Jacob Hoffman's daughter is said to have died at a very young age. According to local folklore, when her fiancé abandoned her for another woman, the broken-hearted girl strung a rope from the attic rafters and hung herself. Her ghostly apparition is now said to wander the third floor, occasionally slamming a bedroom door in bitter anger.

Booted footsteps reverberate throughout the first floor, and in the front parlor where the field surgeons performed their horrific surgery, phantom voices often scream in pain. The apparition of a distinguished older gentleman haunts the dining room, and a mischievous wraith knocks down wine glasses in the kitchen and moves various objects around the inn. Shadowy figures float across the second-floor ballroom, and more than a few guests have experienced the icy touch of a ghostly hand upon their shoulders.

Countless paranormal teams have investigated at the site. A few have captured images displaying formless mists by utilizing infrared camcorders, and found whispered voices imprinted on their digital recorders. Psychics and mediums have been consulted over the years, but none of them have sensed anything aggressive or decidedly evil at the Mansion House. It is their belief that the spirits only want our attention, perhaps to remind us that their young lives were cut tragically short, their life's work left unfinished, and their great sacrifice should never be forgotten.

The Mansion House was one of the first taverns in the Gettysburg area.

22

Iverson's Pits

The Doubleday Inn stands on the site of one of the most lopsided and tragic battles of the Civil War, the area known as Iverson's Pits. Hauntings have been reported here as far back as 1870, only shortly after the nation finally began to heal from its long and bloody internal war. Hired hands working for John Forney's Farm refused to work the fields once the evening settled. The men told of whispered voices calling out in the night. At other times, the farmhands saw shadowy figures that carried muskets prowling the outskirts of the forest, and some described the chilling sound of rebel soldiers shouting out in terror, calling for their mothers with their last, dying breaths. It was at Iverson's Pits that the terrified inhabitants of Gettysburg saw the earliest indications that the dead were not at rest, and the ghostly phenomena continues to this very day.

The Doubleday Inn is the only Gettysburg hotel standing on a battlefield.

Originally part of John Forney's apple orchard, the Doubleday Inn was founded in 1939 by Reverend Abram Longanecker and his wife, Agnus. Abram was an 1898 graduate of the Gettysburg Lutheran Seminary. By Gettysburg standards, the hotel is one of the newer establishments, but it is the only one located on a battlefield site. Its proximity to Iverson's Pits has turned it into a paranormal hotspot. Today, this rustic bed and breakfast is owned and operated by Greg and Sue Rosensteel. The nine-room venue is tastefully furnished with authentic nineteenth-century antiques, but patrons spending the weekend may experience a different kind of living history.

Visitors who stay at the Doubleday Inn and dare to venture out into the misty fields by night often describe a chilling scene; hundreds of white handkerchiefs fluttering in the wind, only inches above the hallowed ground. This ghastly reminder marks the shallow ditch that became a mass gravesite for an entire regiment of Confederate soldiers.

Other guests have encountered young men they assumed were Civil War reenactors, hired to give the hotel some historical authenticity, only to watch them suddenly vanish before their eyes.

One of the housekeepers found herself working the late shift on a crisp October evening. As she turned a corner to enter the second-floor hallway, she encountered the full-bodied apparition of a Confederate soldier. He lifted his hand as if to ask a question, but the young woman shouted out in terror. Two other employees heard the scream and ran up the stairs and into the hallway, but the figure had vanished into thin air. She recovered her composure and described the specter appearing as substantial as a living person. His clothes had been caked with mud and his face covered in soot, but she could describe his uniform and antiquated weaponry in perfect detail.

Employees and guests at the Doubleday Inn report all kinds of paranormal incidents, including streaks of light traveling through the dining room, floating orbs that supply

Visitors at the site of the massacre sometimes see white flags waving across the wheat field.

their own ghostly luminescence, phantom footsteps, the smell of sulfur, loud knocking on bedroom doors, disembodied voices, and even entire conversations between two different departed souls.

One young couple stayed at the inn for two nights while visiting Gettysburg. They left for the day with their room in disarray and returned late that evening to find that their clothing and personal items had been neatly packed back into their suitcases. They enquired of the housekeepers but were assured that hotel employees would never pack a guest's suitcase for them. One can only conclude that some of these spirits have a sense of humor, or perhaps one of them just cannot stand a mess.

The apparition of a young woman in nineteenth-century clothing has been observed roaming the halls of the old inn. One guest described encountering the spirit in the hallway and, assuming the specter was an employee dressed in period clothing, she stopped to compliment the inn on their attention to detail. The mysterious visitor had vanished without a trace.

A middle-aged couple from New York found themselves engaged in conversation with a decorated officer in uniform who wore a trimmed beard and carried an air of terrible sadness. This tragic figure, encountered more than a few times over the years, is believed to be the ghost of General Iverson himself, the man who had commanded the Confederate unit and sent them to their doom.

General Iverson's doomed troops ignored the stone wall on their left, which led to their brutal massacre.

It was the first day of battle on July 1, 1863, and Brigadier General Alfred Iverson had just arrived at the town of Gettysburg with 1,400 soldiers, the North Carolina Brigade composed of the 5th, 12th, 20th, and 23rd Infantries. He was ordered to outflank the Union First Core at Oak Hill, a strategic location on the northernmost point of Seminary Ridge. His brigades formed into lines of battle in the manner that British troops had employed for centuries, marching in strict formation. Roughly 300 yards ahead of Iverson's men stood a copse of trees, and the general was led to believe that Union soldiers were stationed in the field beyond this small patch of forest. He had planned to burst from the woods with muskets blazing and catch the Yankees by surprise. For some unknown reason, he failed to employ an advance line of skirmishers designed to draw enemy fire or sniff out an ambush, a fatal mistake.

Meanwhile, the 12th Massachusetts, known as "Webster's Regiment," were deployed along McPherson's Ridge, where they expected to face waves of Confederate soldiers attacking from the north and west. Joining with two other regiments, they formed the point of an inverted "V," a maneuver known in military parlance as "refusing the line." Utilizing this strategy, they could fend off attacks from either side, as their line could bend back upon itself and create a double line of fire. The first rebel surge came from the east, and the Union lines held. They repelled a subsequent attack from the west, causing the Union line to face northwest and spread across McPherson's Ridge. Exhausted and low on ammunition, the commander instructed his men to conceal themselves behind a stone wall that extended along the crest of the ridge, where they could reload in relative safety. Shortly, they were joined by the Baxter and Robinson Brigades.

General Iverson remained in the rear as his troops marched across the empty field, completely ignoring the stone wall to their left. The Federal troops could not believe their good fortune. They waited until the rebels were less than 50 feet away, then rose to their feet and fired volley after volley into the doomed brigade. Survivors of the massacre described the terrible scene in vivid detail, the air filled with a great cloud of gunpowder as the Yankees mowed down the entire row in a single volley.

According to General Iverson, "Five hundred rebel soldiers marched bravely forward so beautifully aligned and fell dead or wounded in a line as straight as a dress parade." He added: "The men fought nobly, without a single man running away. No greater gallantry was displayed during the war." Shortly after this tragic blunder, Iverson suffered a nervous breakdown and was relieved of command. He was sent home in disgrace to North Carolina and would never see another moment of combat.

Union army survivors described the scene as complete chaos, some rebels being sprayed by the blood of the leading line, then hugging the ground and waving handkerchiefs in surrender as a second volley struck them from the other side of the field. Lieutenant George Bullock of the 23rd North Carolina stated that it was the only time in the entire Civil War that he saw blood flowing so freely that it formed a river along the hillside. Small wonder that this field is haunted.

When the battle ended, the Yankees dug a long trench and buried almost 900 rebels in a mass gravesite, which came to be known as Iverson's Pits. Months later the graves began to settle, forming long, sunken rows that indicated where the bodies had lain. John Forney, owner of the farmland, would later describe a strange phenomenon at Iverson's Pits. In the years that followed, the grass would grow longer and greener above their graves than in any other part of the field.

In 1873, a movement begun in the South by the wives and orphans of the soldiers lost in battle raised enough money to recover and reinter the bodies in North Carolina, but it is very likely that some of the Confederate bodies were never discovered. Perhaps that is the reason so many of these forgotten souls remain here in death, reliving the one-sided battle that took their young lives.

In warfare, the most carefully planned campaigns often descend into complete chaos. Conditions are constantly changing, communication breaks down, and the enemy is always changing plans and location. General Iverson was a haunted man in life; it is not surprising to find his consciousness locked in this place and time, where his ill-fated strategy may have turned the tide of battle and cost his brave young charges their lives. But it seems unfair for him to bear that awful burden until the end of time. Perhaps his tortured soul will someday find the eternal peace he deserves.

At the Doubleday Inn, guests may encounter the ghostly apparition of General Alfred Iverson.

Bibliography

Adelman, G., and Smith, T., *Devil's Den: A History and Guide* (Gettysburg, PA: Thomas Publications, 1997) pp. 26-38

Alleman, B., "Gettysburg's Haunted Battlefield," February 25, 2021, www.civilwarghosts.com

Alleman, M., *At Gettysburg, or What a Girl Saw and Heard of the Battle: A True Narrative* (New York: W. Lake Borland, 1889), pp. 3-45

Allen, G., "Stories from the Wood: The George Weikert Farm," October 18, 2023, www.gettysburgsentinels.com

Audre, A., "Cruel Headmistress, Haunted Orphanage," June 1, 2021, www.truthorscares.com

Bell, C., "What Happened to Gettysburg's Confederate Dead," July 26, 2012, www.wordpress.com

Bitikofer, S., "William Barksdale: Mississippi Fire-Eater," October 23, 2019, www.belleonthebattlefield.wordpress.com

Brkich, V., "Ghost Hunting at the Farnsworth House Inn," October 26, 2016, www.valentinebrkich.com

Brown, P., "Iverson's Pits: 12th Massachusetts Infantry at Gettysburg," July 11, 2014, www.historicaldigression.com

Budnik, R., "The Ghosts of Gettysburg: A Haunted History of a Battlefield," April 7, 2019, www.warhistoryonline.com

Caggiano, G., "Gettysburg Journal 2013: Ghost Hunting at the Grove," August 20, 2013, www.gcaggiano.wordpress.com

Carre, J., "Haunted Cashtown Inn," February 22, 2006, www.hauntedhouses.com; "The Hummelbaugh Farm," May 23, 2019, www.hauntedhouses.com

Chelsie, C., "The Haunted and Historic Fairfield Inn, 1757," August 10, 2003, www.haunts.com

Coleman, C., *Ghosts and Haunts of the Civil War: Authentic Accounts of the Strange and Unexplained* (Nashville, TN: Harper Collins, September 1999), pp. 57-61

Cook, J., "Owners Celebrate Historic Inn's New Chapter," *The Gettysburg Times*, October 24, 2021 (Gettysburg, PA), pp. 4-5

D'Ecclesis, N., "The Most Haunted Bridge in America... Sachs Bridge," March 29, 2021, www.noradecclesis.com

Donley, S. and Donley, M., "Our Haunted Travels: Investigating and Staying at the Cashtown Inn," September 25, 2022, www.ourhauntedtravels.com; "Visiting and Investigating Sachs Covered Bridge," January 9, 2020, www.ourhauntedtravels.com

Dunkelman, M., "Desperate Stand: What the Brickyard Fight Meant at Gettysburg," June 26, 2018, www.historynet.com

Ear, S., "The Lonely Mural," August 15, 2012, www.gettysburgbattlefieldtours.com

Editor, E., "The Battle of Gettysburg: Lee's Invasion of the North," October 29, 2009, www.history.com

Egnatz, E., "A Ghost Named Tennessee," October 25, 2023, www.hauntingsaroundamerica.com

Estep, R., The Fairfield Hauntings: On the Gettysburg Ghost Trail (Charleston, SC: CreateSpace Publishing, February 2018), pp. 51-52, 64-67

Fitzpatrick, M., "A Perfect Storm for the Paranormal: Touring America's Most Haunted Town," *The Guardian*, October 30, 2018 (New York, NY), pp. 13-14

Gardner, K., "The Farnsworth House Inn," *The Frederick News Post*, October 28, 2010, (Frederick, MD), pp. 24-25

"Generals and Villains: The Ghosts of Gettysburg," September 5, 2022, www.usghostadventures.com

Gorlewski, S., "A Visit with the Ghosts of Gettysburg," *The Buffalo News*, October 26, 1999, (Buffalo, NY) pp. 34-35

Greenman, T., "Haunted Gettysburg: True Ghost Stories from Little Round Top, Then and Now," August 9, 2023, www.gothichorrorstories.com

Harding, J., *General John Reynolds & Kate Hewitt: A Tragic Love Story* (Mt. Pleasant, SC: Arcadia Publishing, February 2022), pp. 4-29; "General John Reynolds & Kate Hewitt: A Tragic Love Story," July 5, 2018, www.thegettysburgexperience.com

Hardy, S., "Fairfield Inn to be featured on Discovery Channel's Ghost Lab," *The Waynesboro Record Herald*, October 19, 2019 (Waynesboro, PA), pp. 12-13

"Haunted Farnsworth House Inn," February 18, 2017, www.farnsworthhouseinn.com

Heisey, C., "Tis Like Crushing Life Out of Her: A Gettysburg Love Story," February 14, 2024, www.catholicwitness.org

Henry, M., "A Ghost at Gettysburg: The 20th Maine's Mysterious Encounter," July 11, 2018, www.mb-henry.com; Henry, M., "A Ghost at Gettysburg: Pennsylvania Hall and Civil War Medicine," October 21, 2019, www.mb-henry.com

Hoover, S., "The Farnsworth House at Gettysburg: History and Hauntings," www.usghostadventures.com; Hoover, S., "The History of Haunts at Little Round Top," August 31, 2022, www.usghostadventures.com

Houser, N., "The Spooks of Sachs Bridge," October 25, 2020, www.thepennsylvaniarambler.wordpress.com

Ireland, K., "Sachs Covered Bridge," October 1, 2017, www.thepetitewanderer.com

James, J., "Historical & Haunted Daniel Lady Farm in Gettysburg," July 6, 2022, www.pastlanetravels.com; James, J., "The Dobbin House Tavern: Two+ Centuries of History & Charm," March 29, 2023, www.pastlanetravels.com; "The Cashtown Inn: A Legendary Landmark to Visit in 2024," September 22, 2023, www.pastlanetravels.com

Johnson, V., "Four Haunted Restaurants in Gettysburg," May 20, 2023, www.reverendvsjohnson.medium.com

Jones, T., "The Terrifying Tigers," *The New York Times*, September 13, 2011 (New York, NY), pp.56-57

Karlsie, K., "Hauntings at Sachs Covered Bridge," April 16, 2020, www. subversify.com

Keeney, G., and Keeney, C., "The Mansion House: Our Story," June 2, 2020, www.mansionhouse1757.com

Kessler, J., "Gettysburg Battle Witness Lived in Selinsgrove," *The Daily Item*, March 14, 2011 (Sunbury, PA), pp. 4-5

Knobloch, S., "A Ghost in the Classroom," January 9, 2013, www.walkingamongtheghostsofgettysburg.wordpress.com

Konstam, A., *Civil War Ghost Stories* (San Diego, CA: Thunder Bay Press, November 21, 2005), pp. 72-77

Krenkel, P., "Gettysburg's Welty House Tells a Civil War Story that you Can Touch," January 1, 20024, www.ydr.com

Ktoy, M., "The Story Behind this Haunted Hotel in Pennsylvania is Terrifying," November 19, 2023, www.civilwartalk.com

Laver, K., "A Defense of Ghost Tours in Gettysburg, PA," October 29, 2014, www.thehistorybandits.com

Lavery, K., "The Specter of Gettysburg" October 29, 2014, www.gettysburgcompiler.org

Levy, D., "Gettysburg Orphanage Honored on 150th Anniversary," *The Evening Sun*, May 28, 2016 (York, PA), pp. 18-19

Masino, S., "The Ghosts of Gettysburg," April 8, 2016, www.susanmasino.com

Matsuo, A., "My Experience in Haunted Gettysburg," November 14, 2011, www.alexmatsuo.com

McInvale, C., "The Farnsworth House Inn," January 27, 2020, www.civilwarghosts.com; "Hauntings at Gettysburg College," January 3, 2020, www.civilwarghosts.com

Mingus, S., *The Louisiana Tigers in the Gettysburg Campaign, June–July 1863* (Baton Rouge: LSU Press, 2014), pp. 69-74

Murphy, R., *On Ghosts* (Charleston, SC: CreateSpace, 2016), pp. 1-34; Murphy, R., *On Ghosts: The Spirit World throughout History* (Charleston, SC: CreateSpace, September 2016), pp. 101-3, 134-37

Myers, D., "The ghosts of Gettysburg," July 3, 2003, www.heraldtribune.com

Nesbitt, M., "George Washington's Ghost Saved the Union," December 19, 2019, www.markvnesbitt.wordpress.com; Nesbitt, M., *Ghost of Gettysburg: Spirits, Apparitions and Haunted Places of the Battlefield* (Gettysburg, PA: Second Chance Publications, 2012), pp. 2-100; *Ghost of Gettysburg II: Spirits, Apparitions and Haunted Places of the Battlefield* (Gettysburg, PA: Second Chance Publications, 2011), pp. 2-45, 67-78; "Hidden, Haunted, Hotspots of Gettysburg #5: The Daniel Lady Farm," September 11, 2013, www.markvnesbitt.wordpress.com; "Hidden, Haunted Hotspots of Gettysburg #9: Culp's Hill and Spangler's Spring," October 30, 2019, www.markvnesbitt.wordpress.com; "Hidden, Haunted, Hotspots of Gettysburg #13," January 30, 2020, www.markvnesbitt.wordpress.com

Nesbitt, M. and Chamberlain, J., *Through Blood and Fire at Gettysburg* (Mechanicsburg, PA: Stackpole Books, April 1996), pp. 30-43

Noe, B., "Ghosts of Gettysburg," October 12, 2011, www.nationalgeographic.com

Oester, D., *Ghosts of Gettysburg: Walking on Hallowed Ground* (Lincoln, NE: iUniverse, 2007), pp. 4-25

Parker, T., "Louisiana Tigers During the Civil War," September 11, 2023, www.64parishes.org

Penrose, I.G., "Haunted G-Burg: the Paranormal Pervades Campus," *The Gettyburgian*, November 3, 2014 (Gettysburg, PA), p. 4

Plank, J., "I Went Ghost Hunting in Gettysburg and Forgot my Proton Pack." October 28, 2015, www.pennlive.com

Plum, J., "Haunted Bed and Breakfasts: Slumber with Ghosts at a Spirited Inn," March 24, 2014, www.thetravelchannel.com

Price-Williams, B., "8 Truly Terrifying Ghost Stories that Prove Gettysburg Is the Most Haunted City in Pennsylvania," September 20, 2023, www.onlyinyourstate.com

Priest, J., *Strong Men of the Regiment Sobbed Like Children: John Reynolds' 1 Corps at Gettysburg on July 1, 1863* (El Dorado Hills, CA: Savas Beatie, June 2024), pp. 61-63

"Real Ghost Stories: Gettysburg Battlefield," December 20, 2022, www.sanjoaquinvalleypress.com

Reardon, C., and Vossler, T., *A Field Guide to Gettysburg* (North Carolina: University of North Carolina Press, 2017), pp. 52-63

Reef, C., *Alone in the World: Orphans and Orphanages in America* (Boston: Houghton Mifflin Harcourt, May 2005), pp. 24-32

Riley, J., "Matilda 'Tillie' Pierce," April 2, 2014, www.tilliepierce.com; Riley, J. "The Tillie Pierce House Inn: A Spooky Tale from the Civil War Era," July 19, 2023, www.gettysburgghosttours.com

Rimlinger, E., "Who's There," October 24, 2019, www.baltimoreschild.com

Roberts, N., *Civil War Ghosts and Legends* (London, UK: Metro Books, December 2003), pp. 9-24

Rowland, T., *Strange and Obscure Stories of the Civil War* (NY, New York: Skyhorse, 2011)

Rudy, J., "Gettysburg College & The Battle of Gettysburg: A Civil War Walking Tour," September 6, 2013, www.gettysburg.edu

Russel, N. "Ghosts of Sachs Bridge," October 28, 2019, www.gypsyjournalrv.com

Schlosser, S., "Haunted Sachs Bridge," May 20, 2022, www.seschlosser.com

Smith, T., "The Rose Farm: The Bloodiest Farm in America," December 27, 2022, www.civilwartalk.com

"The Spirit of Spangler's Spring," October 21, 2018, www.thepennsylvaniarambler.wordpress.com

Uszak, E., "Blood, Sweat, and Tears: The Rose Family and the Battle of Gettysburg," December 23, 2021, www.gettysburgcompiler.org

Uzal W., *The Pennsylvania Reserves in the Civil War: A Comprehensive History* (North Carolina: McFarland & Company, 2014), p. 373-375.

Walters, M., "Owner Tries to Sell Tillie Pierce House," *The Gettysburg Times*, June 2, 2011 (Gettysburg, PA), pp. 5-6

Zimmerman, N., "The Spirits of Stevens Hall," November 18, 2017, www.frightfind.com

Zurn, A., "Haunted Lancaster: The Ghost of General Reynolds," October 1, 2019, www.unchartedlancaster.com

About the Author

Barry Corbett spent six years as the lead investigator for Boston Paranormal, one of the longest-running ghost-hunting groups in the Boston area. Established in 2005, they handled both private cases and public investigations, exploring more than 150 haunted sites throughout New England. As he conducted historical research for active locations, Barry discovered a wealth of stories encompassing New England's rich, colonial history, from the Puritan settlers at Plymouth Colony, through the witch trials at Old Salem Village, and to the beginnings of the Revolutionary War.

Combining his love of photography with a lifelong fascination with ghosts, Barry published his first book with Fonthill Media, *The Boston Paranormal Archives*, a visual sampling of haunted Boston and a fascinating collection of tragic tales, restless spirits, and American history.

He is also a professional cartoonist, with panel cartoons appearing in *Reader's Digest*, *American Legion Magazine*, *Barron's*, *Lacrosse Magazine*, *True West Magazine*, *Kid Zones*, *Prospect Magazine*, *Medical Economics*, *First for Women*, *Fantasy & Science Fiction*, *The Chicago Loop News*, *The Valley News*, *Christianity Today*, and *The Artist's Magazine*.

Barry released his first book in 2006. *Embrace the Pun* is a collection of pun-based panel cartoons. He followed that up with *Revenge of the Pun* and *The Pun Rides Again*.

Revenge of the Pun won a Bronze Medal at the 2011 IPPY Awards, presented by *Independent Publisher Magazine* and a Silver Medal at *ForeWord Magazine's* 2010 Book of the Year Awards.

Kitty Nirvana: The First Ginger & Shadow Collection was released in 2008 and won a Silver Medal at the IPPY Awards. *It's a Cat Thing*, the second collection, was released in 2012.

Barry has published comic books under the imprint Griffin Comics; *Gormon*, a science fiction mini-series, *Star Crossed*, a romantic fantasy, and *Terminal Velocity*, an autobiographical series about a childhood tragedy, his adventures playing ice hockey, and his comical attempts to become a skydiver, which he later compiled into a 110-page graphic memoir.

He has written short stories for science fiction magazines *Bards & Sages Quarterly* and *The Colored Lens*. His latest comic strip creation, *The League of Evil, Mad Scientists* appears in Barry's monthly comics newsletter, "Two-Fisted Tales," which is co-authored by fellow cartoonist Brian Codagnone.

A graduate of the Vesper George School of Art in Boston, Barry forged a career in graphic design and later transitioned to full time writing and cartooning. Barry resides with his wife, Margaret, in North Reading, Massachusetts, where he continues to research the paranormal.